table inspirations

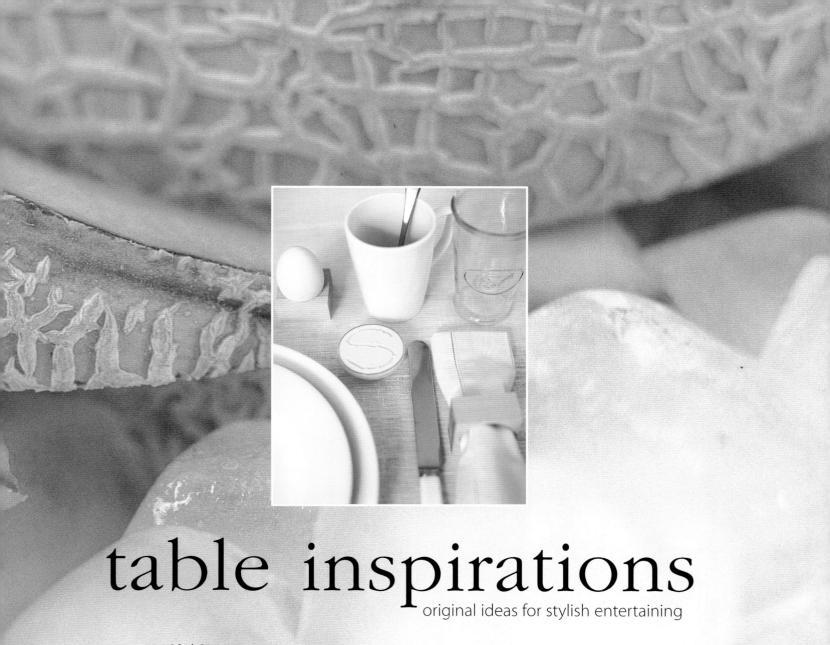

table inspirations

original ideas for stylish entertaining

RYLAND
PETERS
& SMALL
London New York

emily chalmers

photography by david brittain

Designer Catherine Randy
Senior editor Sophie Bevan
Location research Emily Chalmers, Kate Brunt,
Sarah Hepworth
Production Patricia Harrington
Art director Gabriella Le Grazie
Publishing director Alison Starling

Stylist Emily Chalmers

First published in the United States in 2001
by Ryland Peters & Small, Inc.
519 Broadway, 5th Floor
New York, NY 10012
www.rylandpeters.com

Library of Congress Cataloging-in-Publication Data

Chalmers, Emily.
  Table inspirations : original ideas for stylish
entertaining / Emily Chalmers ; photography by David
Brittain.-- pbk. ed.
      p. cm.
  Includes index.
  ISBN 1-84172-918-3
  1. Table setting and decoration. 2. Entertaining. I.
Title.
  TX879.C47 2005
  642'.8--dc22
                                    2004020325

Printed in China.

contents

introduction

Whatever the occasion—be it festive or everyday, grand or intimate—it's easy to create an atmosphere that will make your guests feel relaxed, happy, and welcome at the table.

Whether is it a birthday buffet for ten guests, a family group of six sitting down for Christmas dinner, or an intimate table for two to celebrate an anniversary—setting a table is all about entertaining your guests. What makes the occasion special is the choice, the combination and the positioning of china, glassware, flowers, candles, and linen.

When buying flowers, carefully consider the shapes and colors that would best decorate the table and surrounding area. Pop placecards at each setting to make the guests feel special—when you are pushed for time, these need only be squares of paper dropped into empty drinking glasses or wedged under a little pebble at the edge of each plate. And there are plenty of ways that linen and flatware can be attractively displayed—fold the napkin around it and tie it with ribbon, or place a folded napkin flat under each dinner plate with the flatware sitting to one side.

The aim of this book is to illustrate that it is the little details that make all the difference. Modern mealtimes tend to be informal, so there is no need to feel confined by the old "rules"—a table can still look stylish without sticking to a more conventional setting, as long as it remains well considered and orderly. The examples given in this book are here to inspire and excite—mix them with your own ideas and, most of all, have fun!

above and right Practical ideas are often the best: an old glass brick makes an interesting holder for an altar candle, and frozen slices of lime are a colorful and cooling ingredient for a refreshing summer drink.
opposite Simple and orderly, while still being decorative, this table setting is ideal for a casual meal with friends.

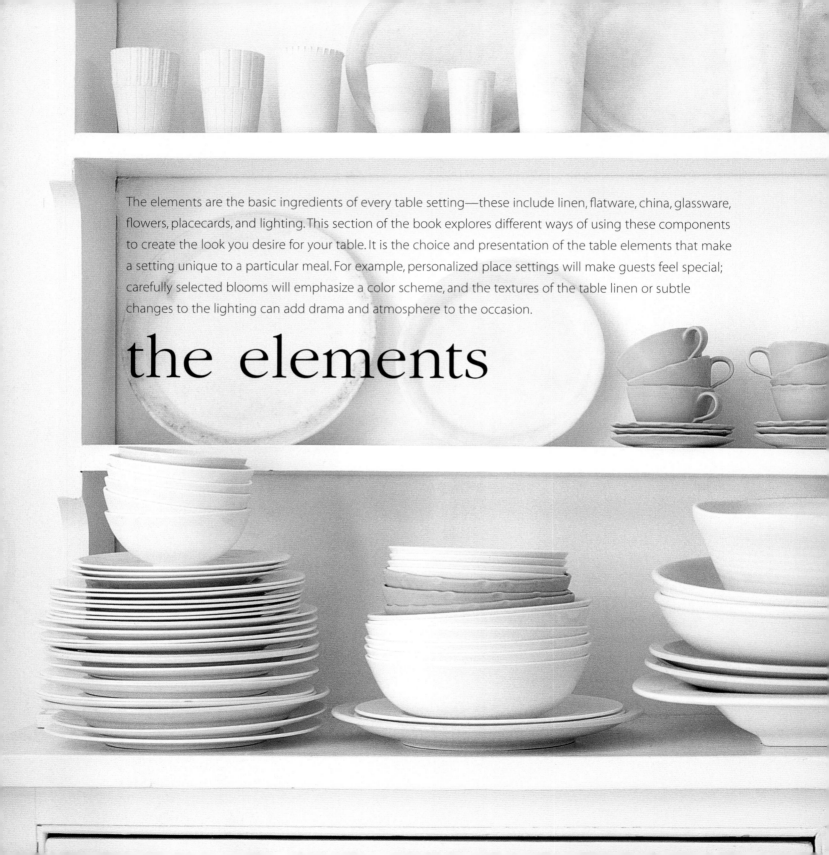

The elements are the basic ingredients of every table setting—these include linen, flatware, china, glassware, flowers, placecards, and lighting. This section of the book explores different ways of using these components to create the look you desire for your table. It is the choice and presentation of the table elements that make a setting unique to a particular meal. For example, personalized place settings will make guests feel special; carefully selected blooms will emphasize a color scheme, and the textures of the table linen or subtle changes to the lighting can add drama and atmosphere to the occasion.

the elements

Cups, plates, and bowls are perhaps the most obvious elements of a table setting. There are many styles, colors, and textures to choose from, so play around with different combinations.

cups, plates, and bowls

The cups, plates, and bowls you choose depend very much on the food and drinks you are serving and the style of the meal. Some occasions call for a large pasta dish, others warrant dinner plate, bread-and-butter plate, and soup bowl—and there are many options for occasions that require no china settings at all.

Good, basic white utility china is indispensable. Plates can be used to eat off, to serve from, or as "mats" for other pieces. Bowls are good for soup, pasta, and salad, as well as for dessert. And cups or glasses can be used for drinks, desserts, and flowers. The variations are almost endless. Pretty, dainty china is also fun to own—try mixing and matching old teacups and saucers for a traditional English tea. Use a special teacup for sugar cubes and a floral cream pitcher to display flowers.

Serving bowls always come in handy, and you can never have too many. They are excellent for a formal meal, but can also be used with floating candles or flower heads for a more relaxed

above It's great to have tall stacks of everyday china to choose from. Invest in a plain white, good-quality set and gradually add other colors and styles that take your fancy.
right A beautifully proportioned teacup needn't be used only for drinking tea—it makes an excellent home for a pretty flower, too! Lay it on top of a stack of plain china for an interesting display. It can be put to one side once the meal has begun.

left There's no need to stick to matching sets of china. Soft pastel colors look good all mixed together. Use a soft-green cup on a baby-blue saucer and stack them on top of white or pale-pink plates and bowls.

below This simple ceramic version of a coffee filter makes a stylish addition to a breakfast-table setting. Look out for individual teapots and juicers, too, so your guests can help themselves.

left A simple small bowl placed on top of a neutral napkin is used here to make an individual place setting. Nutmegs, small washed pebbles, or single flower heads can be added to give a personal touch. The combination of linen, ceramic, and metal used here on a dark, thick wooden table top is striking, and the overall look is softened with bright flowers.
above Choose organically shaped dishes made from natural materials. You can never have enough tiny platters to hold olives, rock salt, roughly ground black pepper, and a selection of nuts and seeds to nibble on with cocktails before dinner.

Make the most of your table elements: keep glassware clean and bright; carefully stack china at a setting; and choose vessels that are dual purpose to display and serve food and drink.

this page, main **Simple clear glass bowls are an invaluable element of a practical kitchen. Use them to mix in, bake in, and serve from.**
below right **The floral decoration on this elegant china helps to soften the otherwise cold look of the setting, and stacking all three pieces creates interesting layers.**

occasion. Stemmed bowls and dishes are great for displaying fruit, but will look equally good at a Christmas table, full of colorful glass balls. Or why not mix the fruit with the decorations?

Keep a lookout for china versions of other tableware—ceramic coffee filters are practical and stylish, and often less expensive than electrical gadgets or large glass cafetières. You can also get ceramic fruit juicers that will look good at a breakfast table.

If a certain piece of china catches your eye, don't worry about having to buy a full set; keep it as a special individual item that can

be mixed with other pieces or used on its own. If in doubt, try to stick to mixing either color or pattern, so the table never looks too cluttered. Pairs of china can be used effectively, too, such as bowls to hold floating candles or dishes to offer rock salt and coarsely ground black pepper.

Look for one-off pieces—it may be an interesting decorative dish that you have picked up on your travels, or an old silver tray handed down in the family. The dish could be perfect holding a large altar candle surrounded by pebbles as a centerpiece to a table; the tray might be great for a birthday buffet, piled with olives sitting on a bed of large green leaves.

The main rule with china is to play around and go with what looks right. If you don't have enough pieces to lay formal settings for everyone, then mix and match different sets or use wooden bowls and napkins for salad, bread, and other extras—there is no rule that you have to eat from china plates and drink from china cups! Wooden platters, tin pots, glass bowls—this is where it is easy to add character and express individuality within the table setting. Look for different materials—these could be your inspiration for a special occasion. Glass plates are an inexpensive way to pad out a dinner set and sit well between pieces of china. Remember that

below left Build up textures: start with a roughly woven table runner or placemat and juxtapose it against plain linen napkins and soft cool soapstone dishes. Food elements such as nuts, raisins, or dried fruit make a stylish table snack and add to the mix of surface textures.

below A lacquer tray provides a good base for a modern layered setting. Glass plates show up colors and enhance the look. Tiny individual bottles of drink and foil-wrapped cookies and candy give a quirky touch.

left Tin plates and recycled cans, simple salad servers, and large wooden platters are all interesting, inexpensive additions to a table.

below Small wooden bowls look lovely in a tall stack and come in handy for individual starters or bowls of nuts to place at each setting. Wood looks great on a warm-colored tablecloth—perfect for a Thanksgiving or Halloween meal.

special large plates, dishes, and trays can always be used as "lay" plates—these are not for eating from, but rather act to define individual settings and make an interesting first layer at each place.

Use large shells to hold nuts, or papier-mâché bowls for bread. A marble bowl could house a single floating gloriosa head or some sliced exotic fruit—use your imagination!

Mix and match different materials for drinking vessels, too. Red wine and colored fruit juice look great in silver or pewter cups and goblets. And their reflective surfaces will create interesting effects around the table. Ceramic cups will also work well if they are in keeping with the rest of the tableware.

Mix materials—ceramic, wood, glass, tin, stone—and lay them over different textures, such as lacquer, cloth, and woven matting.

glasses and decanters

Clean, bright glassware adds a sparkling touch to any table setting. Collect whatever takes your fancy and enjoy mixing and matching.

Glasses, bottles, pitchers, and decanters are very versatile table elements. In addition to being used for drinks, interesting pieces can be used to display flowers and hold votive and floating candles. Cut, colored, recycled, thick, dainty—there are so many styles available, but the most important thing is to make sure all your glassware is as clean and shiny as possible. Remove stubborn water stains by soaking in vinegar, and change flower water regularly.

Scour secondhand stores and antique markets for one-off pieces of colored cut glass—they might just give that extra-special touch that your table top needs. If any of these favorite pieces get chipped, there's no need to throw them away. Simply file away any dangerous surfaces and reuse them to hold candles and votives or candy and sugar cubes.

Plain pieces of drinking glassware can be jazzed up with temporary stick-on decorations or tattoos, or

opposite left Tiny pieces of edible flower petals have been set in ice for a pretty summer drink.

opposite right These tall glasses have been rubbed with lemon juice and dipped in a bowl of decorative sugar to give them a special crystallized rim.

below This green glass picks out the colors of the flowers and candles. A big glass jar provides a good container for pastel-colored bonbons.

right These plain heavy-duty glasses have been given a special touch with the addition of simple stick-on bindis—readily available from stores selling Asian products.

Plain, recycled, etched, colored, cut ... mix pieces together
for a timeless and eclectic look on your table top.

use jewelry wire to attach sequins, tiny gemstones, or small buttons around plain water glasses. Flat jewel-like decorations and glitter confetti can also be stuck onto glassware with nontoxic adhesive. There are lots of different etching and transfer kits that you can have fun with, too.

Don't be afraid to mix old and new pieces of glassware, and different colors and shapes can also look very effective side by side on the table. Choose the odd piece in a complementary color to dot around a table and enhance a particular scheme.

Because of the transparent quality of most table glassware, it is the element that can be most easily dressed up or down to complement the mood of a particular occasion. Make the most of this feature— fill bottles with colored water purely for decoration. Use large clear glasses to present interesting and exotic fruit salads, and so on. Think how different you can make a table top appear by substituting cut glass with smooth plain glass pieces, or by filling glasses with cranberry juice instead of water at each place setting. A few candles placed in antique

above left Scour antique stores and markets for special pieces. This old pitcher would never be strong enough to carry liquids, but it makes a dainty holder for sugar stirrers.
above These basic handmade glasses are ideal for serving juice or yogurt at the breakfast table.

left Collect interesting pieces of glassware to mix and match on your table top. Special wineglasses can also be used for fruit juice or sparkling water, and need not be kept back purely for elegant dining.

above Traditional old-fashioned glass milk bottles make interesting holders for drinks instead of a pitcher on the table. Little glass mugs and cups make pleasing vessels for cold drinks.

Choose clear tall glasses to show off bright cocktails and use simple glass votives to serve rows of vodka gelatine. Perfect for a party setting!

opposite Use etching spray and stencils to build up an alphabet on a set of inexpensive glasses. This romantic arrangement is perfect for a Valentine's table setting or anniversary celebration. Cranberry juice and a single rose petal add to the theme.

left Glassware can look striking against stone and metal. This simple votive is presented individually on a square candleholder topped with an aluminum coaster. Look for suitable shapes to build up individual settings. A sprig of mint and a delicate flower head make this little offering extra-special.

colored cut-glass wineglasses will add a very deca-dent quality to an otherwise plain spread.

Collect one-off decanters to add a twist to the table top—red wine not only tastes better when it is presented in a decanter, but looks better, too. Introduce decanters for any colorful drinks you are serving—diluted lime juice and fruit juices. Decanters can also be used for table-top flowers; even a narrow-necked vessel will hold a couple of beautiful stems of orchids and look elegant on your table. If you want to get really creative or exploit a dramatic color scheme, fill your decanters with diluted food coloring and add coordinating flowers for a really vibrant and fun display—perfect for a party or occasion such as New Year's Eve.

The key is to experiment and think laterally—old glass milk bottles make great vases and are even good as decanters at the right setting. Likewise, an interesting vase might be a good substitute for a decanter—as long as it pours well! Votive holders can double as little drinking glasses, just as interesting glasses can be used to hold candles. Try placing a glass plate on top of a glass vase to create a stemmed dish for a centerpiece—just play around!

above Place knives and forks in interesting envelopes for guests to pick out from a large jar or a decorative galvanized bucket.

right For an informal setting, group pieces of flatware together in clear glass utility jars—ideal for a large breakfast or brunch, when guests can help themselves according to what they choose to eat.

opposite left Mixing and matching older styles of flatware can be very effective. For example, varied styles of antique silver are perfect for classic occasions like a Christmas tea party or a Mother's Day lunch.

opposite below right Plain knives and forks are brought to life with special decorative touches for a buffet-style party.

flatware

There are many elegant styles of flatware available, but you can create as great an impact by stylish presentation of the humblest pieces.

The presentation of flatware is a useful way to add to the decoration of your table without investing in expensive silverware sets. For a formal sit-down meal, you will probably opt for a traditional setting, such as those shown in the guide to settings (see pages 130–137). However, there are many other elegant ways to lay knives, forks, and spoons.

Buffet tables offer great scope: flatware can be laid out in rows and tied together in many attractive ways. Florists often stock wired decorations, that are perfect for tying individual sets of flatware. Alternatively, try making your own with a length of wire secured to a flower head or other small decorative object. Make your flatware festive, too, and decorate a Christmas place setting with a shiny gold ball tied to the flatware with a rich red ribbon.

napkins and tablecloths

With just a little thought and imagination, napkins, tablecloths, and runners can be an easy way to add color and texture to your setting.

Tablecloths and runners can quickly transform the look of a table and are often a great source of inspiration for the design of the rest of the setting. Apart from being required for practical reasons to protect the table top, they are also an excuse to introduce areas of interesting color or texture or to dictate the best areas to lay individual settings.

Napkins are relatively inexpensive to buy, and it is easy to collect an interesting selection. They are also very simple to make, which means there really are limitless opportunities to be creative with them. If you are making your own table runner or tablecloth from a piece of special fabric, make sure there is enough left over to make a set of napkins or at least to edge some plain ones to

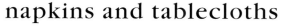

above left Pick up remnants of satin lining to enhance your table palette. This piece in shocking pink looks great against the shades of green in this layered setting.

above There are many decorative objects that can be used as napkin rings, such as this flower hairband that makes a pretty addition at a tea table. Buy a set in different colors to spread interest around the table—the bands can double as gifts for guests to take home after the meal.

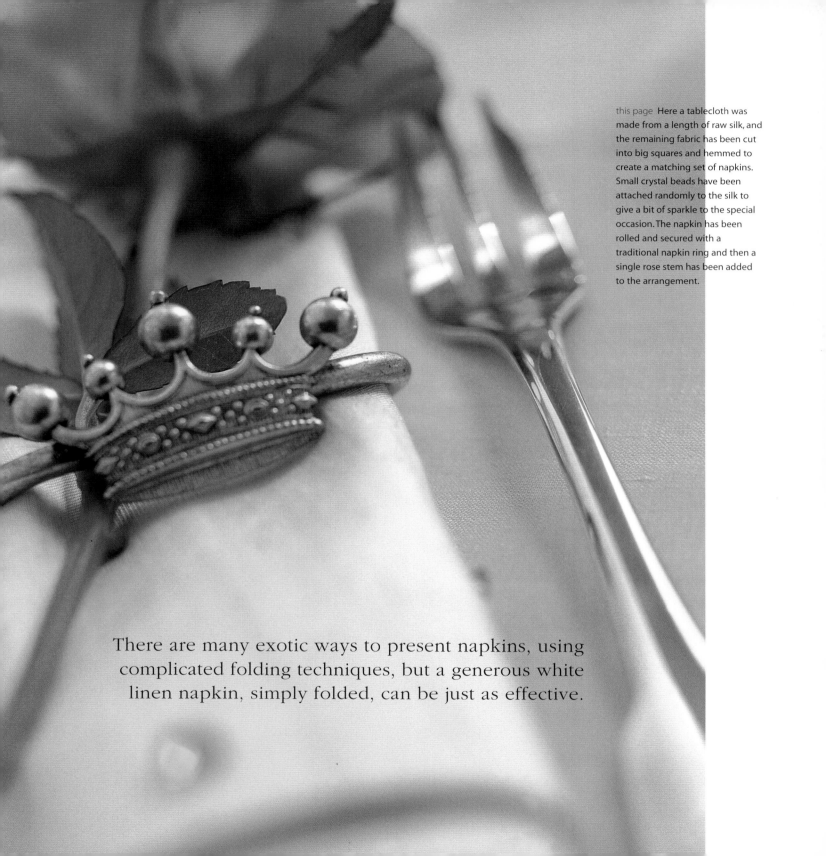

There are many exotic ways to present napkins, using complicated folding techniques, but a generous white linen napkin, simply folded, can be just as effective.

below A paper-napkin holder found at a yard sale makes an interesting and practical addition to a casual breakfast table top.

right Shades of orange and yellow will brighten up a setting. Choose table linen to coordinate with your china, food, or the general dining-room decor, mixing up different textures on the table.

far right An Asian-style table setting has been given color and texture with satin table linen.

match. Whether you are buying or making napkins, the only criterion should be that you can easily wash them (apart from paper napkins, of course!).

The way you display napkins on the table can be as important as the napkins themselves, and will add character to your special occasion. We have all seen intricately folded napkins—making shapes, such as swans, miters, peacock tails— this can be interesting. But you needn't be skilled in the art of origami in order to present a napkin effectively. While traditionally the napkin is positioned on the left of the setting, it is fun to think of new and interesting alternatives. Sometimes a dinner plate will sit well on a napkin folded lengthwise. Sometimes the napkin acts as a good divider between two pieces of china and, if you choose your colors carefully, you can create some interesting layers by laying the napkin in a stack of plates and bowls at each setting. Napkins look good with flatware, too, especially for a buffet occasion, when they can all be wrapped together with a length of pretty ribbon—or with ivy at Christmas time, for example.

this page Personalizing an boiled egg at a breakfast table will organize your guests and bring a smile to their faces first thing in the morning. This inflatable egg cup is also good at a children's party.

opposite left A piece of birthday cake and little party gifts have been put into these takeout containers to give away at a children's party. Liquid cake icing has been used to write each guest's name on their individual box, which was then secured with colored string and tied to a balloon.

opposite right These little acrylic cubes are ideal for holding placecards to sit neatly at each place setting.

placecards

There are numerous ways to create personalized place settings, and the more inspirational you are, the more special your guests will feel when they come to sit down at the table.

When you are coming up with ideas for placecards, try to incorporate elements from the existing setting, such as using a cocktail stick to flag a card in an empty glass or, for a special breakfast or supper-time treat, carve an initial in an individual butter pat or write a name on a boiled egg.

Alternatively, create special individual arrangements around a handwritten placecard using found objects that reflect the setting of the meal, such as a flower petal to echo the floral theme of the decorations or a pebble from the beach or garden when dining alfresco. Another idea is to write names on old-fashioned luggage or price labels and then tie them to the handles of knives and forks at each setting or to a single decorative bloom. Labeled table gifts are a good way to mark each place, and a personalized label will turn the simplest flower stem laid on each plate or napkin into a special gift for each guest.

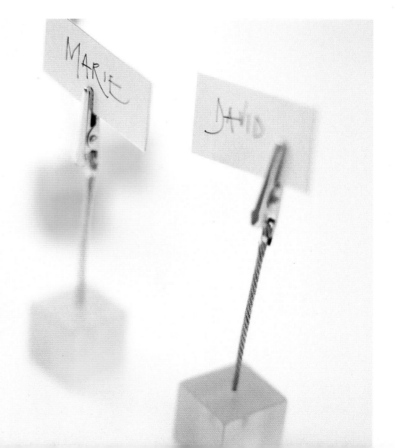

below A plant tag is used at each place setting for this children's party. A miniature cactus has been carefully planted in an acrylic pot as a gift for each child to take home after the event.

right There are many styles of placecard holders available today. This set of tiny handbags is particularly quirky. Write your guests' names in colored ink to coordinate with the rest of the setting.

far right A plain brown luggage tag sits happily strung around this denim napkin. Tying the fork into the bundle is ideal for a buffet or barbecue.

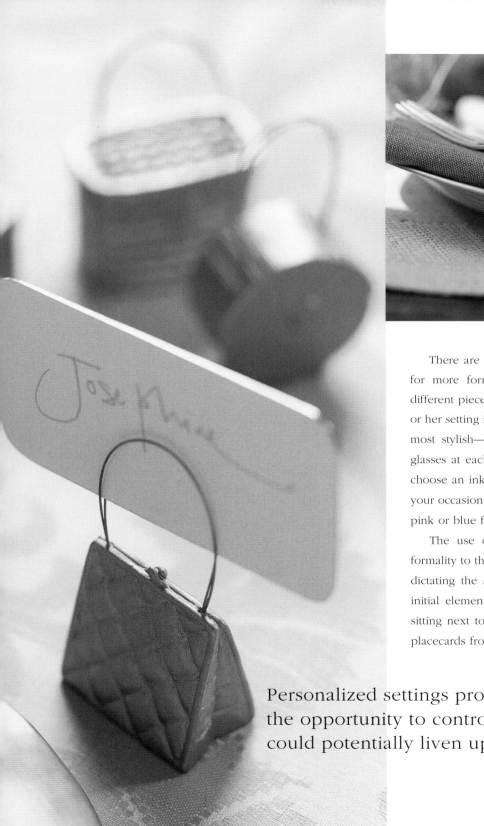

There are also plenty of placecard holders that can be bought for more formal occasions. Look for sets that include slightly different pieces along the same theme, so each guest feels that his or her setting is unique. Or—the simplest option can often look the most stylish—drop handwritten cards into empty wine or water glasses at each place. When you are writing names on the cards, choose an ink color that will coordinate with the color scheme of your occasion, such as metallic gold for a Christmas dinner, or pale pink or blue for a christening or baby shower.

The use of placecards will always bring a slight sense of formality to the overall setting, in the way that you, as the host, are dictating the seating arrangements. But this in itself will add an initial element of surprise as your guests discover who they are sitting next to. Why not play on this idea and get guests to pick placecards from a hat to choose their neighbors at the table?

Personalized settings provide you, as the host, with the opportunity to control seating arrangements that could potentially liven up the meal!

placemats and coasters

As the potential building blocks of a table setting, placemats and coasters are very important elements, bringing interest to an otherwise plain surface.

From a practical point of view, placemats and coasters protect the table surface from moisture and scratches, and may be required to act as insulation for hot plates and bowls placed on top. They also have a decorative function, providing the opportunity to introduce different colors, textures, and materials to your table top.

In addition, placemats help determine a specific area for a single setting, and they can be important elements within a layering theme at each place. You may want to use a mat as a base color and build upward with a pile of china elements, or perhaps you would like to see the interesting textures of a square of felt underneath a large glass dinner plate.

Placemats can be made from a wide variety of materials: fabric, cork, and rattan provide interesting textures, as do slate, leather, and rubber. Slate mats allow for another level of interest: chalk writes well on slate and could be used to personalize place settings or to label mats carrying condiments or dishes for

above left These heavily textured circular sisal placemats look great in an outdoor setting, particularly with the contrasting smooth surface of this soapstone dish. Extend the theme with sisal baskets to hold flatware and serve textured rustic bread and smooth nuts and seeds for your guests to nibble on.

above Here, again, we see groups of textures working well together. The loosely woven raffia table runner has a fantastic fringed edge. A small square of linen has been sewn into a coaster.

Accentuate textures and shapes on your table top by choosing placemats and coasters in interesting materials. Use rough sisal, spongy cork, raw linen, uneven slate—and have fun!

this page Coasters can be found in all manner of fabrics. These elegant squares are made from beaded material that adds a touch of decadence to the setting. They are great for special festive occasions— gold at Christmas or pearl beads for a dainty Mother's Day tea table. It is also fun to play around with unexpected objects—inexpensive squares of cork can be used as placemats or cut down to coaster size, and scraps of old slate look great as a background to a contemporary table setting.

right These placemats and coasters have been made from inexpensive gray felt. The felt was cut into squares with sharp scissors and then the corners were rounded off to give an organic feel to an otherwise austere setting. A hole was cut into each mat as a decorative touch. Fabrics such as this work particularly well on a thick glass table top.

below These brightly colored rubber placemats look striking at a children's party or fun celebration, and make a good base for a layered setting. Mix and match primary colors over the table top for a sunny feel.

left This bright, woven mat looks great outside on a sunny day and works well against the distressed paintwork of outdoor furniture.
below A leaf makes an interesting and unusual base for this watermelon. There is an increasingly good choice of large exotic leaves on the market—just check that they are not poisonous before you use them!

guests to help themselves. A large wooden dish could also be used as a placemat and might be an excellent "container" for the other elements set down, in a similar way to an individual tray. Some plates are large enough to be used as placemats themselves.

Coasters are like small placemats—again serving for protection and for decoration. If it is necessary to use coasters, it is worth putting some thought into choosing them. Again, there is an opportunity here to enter into the total theme of the setting with the appropriate colors and textures.

It is often possible to pick up coasters that match readymade placemats or napkins, but it is by no means necessary to use a matching set. As with placemats, squares and circles of leather or organic shapes cut from felt can look wonderful on a table top. Or use remnants of favorite fabrics—a spare napkin will usually cut down to a full set of matching coasters. Special ceramic tiles can be bought singly and mixed and matched together to create an interesting set of coasters (add a square of felt to the base of any rough surface). Squares of colorful carpet or rubber or linoleum flooring (often handed over as sample pieces) are great for placemats and coasters at a children's table. And small circular cosmetic mirrors are ideal for sitting under shot glasses at a party. The possibilities are almost endless!

candles and lighting

Playing around with different lighting solutions is one of the quickest ways to change the mood of your table to suit the occasion.

Pay special attention to the lighting—both natural and artificial—of your dining area. A table set in a large bay window surrounded with sunlight will feel bright and airy, while an abundance of small table-top candles will bring a feeling of festivity and intimacy to the meal.

Candles are an obvious lighting solution at a dining table, but they can be used in many imaginative and unexpected ways. Look for unusual candleholders—you needn't go to any expense, as you probably have suitable bowls and jars around the house that you have never thought of employing for lighting!

Traditional votive candles are an inexpensive and versatile option, and make a welcome addition to the table. They can be placed by each setting, in

above These votive holders can be anchored with suction pads to any flat clean surface. They are particularly effective at a window, reflecting spots of light around the room.
right Tiny candles are effective at individual settings. The candle on the right is made from clear gel that burns in a similar way to wax.

Choose candles and lighting carefully to illuminate your table setting. There are many ways of incorporating these extra elements into your chosen theme, whether for practicality or pure decoration.

this page, main **Buy bundles of candles that catch your eye—you can never have too many!**

below A storm lantern or hurricane lamp is an excellent way of lighting an outdoor setting. Try collecting brightly colored flower heads from the yard to drop into the glass jar around the base of the candle. If you don't have a table-top lantern, a large vase or pitcher could be used for a light—just make sure the candle flame stays well clear of any surfaces.

rows across the table, and scattered on surrounding surfaces, giving spots of light all around the room.

There are many types of candle available, and even more ways of displaying them. Try sticking standard dinner candles or tapers upright in a bowl filled with sand or coarse salt. Or a single wide pillar candle surrounded by decorative elements, such as flower heads or pebbles, can be as effective as a cluster of smaller candles.

It is fun, too, to be inventive with electric lighting. Try placing a line of tree lights lengthwise along a party table to add spots of light, or attach an

above **These galvanized buckets contain candles scented with citronella—a natural insect repellent—which makes them the obvious choice for a garden or balcony party. Place them around the edges of a balcony to illuminate a barbecue scene.**
left **These little ceramic cups make excellent holders for votives and look particularly effective placed together in a row along a wooden shelf or mantelpiece. Made from fine china, they give a softer, warmer glow than glassware would.**

artificial flower head close to each beam for a colorful, funky setting. Tree lights also work well in a cluster and could be hung from a hook on the wall or placed in a colored glass or plastic serving bowl for an interesting centerpiece.

If you have both, mix electric lighting with candlelight for your occasion. A string of colorful lights hanging over a doorway, around a window frame, or left in a cluster in the far corner of the room will look particularly effective if they echo the glow of votive candles in colored glass bowls on the table. The lighting can also be spread out and into the yard if you have your table by a set of French doors or a big window. Even if the weather is bad, lanterns or multicolored outdoor tree lights can be grouped outside to give an extended colorful glow. If you want to be really clever, mix electric lighting and candlelight for an unusual

above Tiny tin votive holders light up a modern table setting. Placed here between the guests' placemats, they create glowing lines across the table. For a more informal setting or an outdoor party, you could use recycled tincans and punch holes in the sides.
left Candlemaking kits are widely available and homemade candles bring a special charm to your table. Practically any vessel is suitable for a candle pot—these little oriental cups look sweet with coordinating colored wax in them.

above **Whether indoors or outside, a row of Chinese paper lanterns suspended from coordinating pink ribbon looks festive strung above a buffet table.**

right **There are plenty of lanterns available to buy, but it is also fun to make your own from recycled jars and tincans. Remove labels from glass jars for a clear glow, and punch holes in clean tincans to see dots of light. Simply wind a piece of wire securely around the top of the jar or can, make a "handle," and attach them to a branch.**

You can never have enough lanterns! If you plan to entertain in the backyard, make sure you have a good stock of lighting options that won't blow out at the first sign of a breeze.

Electric lighting can be a fun alternative to candles, and tree lights aren't just for Christmas! These colorful chili lights look great hanging behind a warmly colored table, at Halloween or Thanksgiving, for example.

centerpiece—why not wind mini tree lights in a circle around a bowl of floating candles?

It is important to look after candles, particularly if they are the long-lasting variety, such as larger altar candles or floor-standing models. For a large candle, try to keep it burning no longer than two hours at the first use—this usually means even burning and is good to start it off. Always watch that wicks don't get too long—this will create a tall flame that can blacken any nearby paintwork over time. Trim wicks to approximately quarter of an inch for best burning potential. And try to keep candles away from drafts: a draft will speed up a candle's burning time and cause irregular burning.

below An interesting arrangement has been made here with a glass bowl containing tree lights arranged around a glitter ball. This bowl has then been positioned inside another glass dish of colored water. Dilute food coloring to create a color that coordinates with the rest of the setting, and take care to keep the electrical cables and bulbs away from the water.

below Dainty single stems have been carefully put together to pick out the pinks and whites in this table setting. Cluster groups of vases of different shapes and sizes for added interest. The butterflies give a special decorative touch.

right Single flower heads can look wonderfully elegant sitting in individual vases—votive holders will work just as well. Cymbidium orchid flowers are extremely effective for this look.

opposite left A single bright gloriosa lily flower is as effective as a whole bunch. Float the flower head in a green bowl to make the colors really stand out.

opposite right Bright artificial flower heads look great on fake grass for a kitsch display.

flowers and plants

Flowers are an obvious way to spruce up your table top for a mealtime or party. There are so many blooms and types of foliage available to choose from—from exotic and unusual species, such as birds-of-paradise, ginger, and anthurium, to more humble, cottage-garden flowers, like lavender and daisies—it is hard to know where to begin.

If you are working to a budget, you will find there is no need to spend too much money on expensive flowers. A few carnation heads floating in a central bowl of water can look as interesting and attractive as a more extravagant orchid. Or, to make your flowers go a long way, try floating petals in individual glass bowls at each setting—votive holders or shot glasses make excellent small vases and are ideal for this purpose. Single flower heads will also look good dotted around the table, and cymbidium orchids are perfect for this look. Another inexpensive idea is to stick to using foliage: choose exotic leaves or tie strands of long grass carefully around napkins or glasses.

Choose flowers and plants carefully for the occasion—to enhance the atmosphere and to strengthen or pick out areas of color in your table setting.

above Think carefully about the vases you choose: here, smooth rounded shapes in matt and shiny finishes contrast with the rough textures and strong lines of the table and runner. The neutral tones offset the single, bright stems of orchids perfectly.

left Single sweet-pea flower heads floating in tiny glass bowls—what could be simpler? These holders can be stacked to create an attractive and highly original decoration for the table.

When buying flowers, remember that a single stem can be as effective and eye-catching as an extravagant mixed bouquet.

Fruit and vegetables can also be usefully employed in place of flowers to bring a slightly different decorative look to an occasion. Alternatively, try using whole plants on the table in place of cut flowers. For instance, orchid plants are more readily available nowadays and can be bought relatively inexpensively and then used again and again. At a more informal setting, place gerbera plants in recycled tincans for a modern fresh look on the table. And miniature cacti are fun planted individually in jars at each place setting for a children's party or unconventional gathering.

Carry floral themes around the dining area—there's no need to restrict decorations to the table. Gather unused pitchers and vases from the kitchen, plant them with blooms to match your color scheme, and spread them all around the house, wherever your guests can appreciate them.

Flowers also make wonderful table gifts, so treat your guests with individual mini bouquets at the table. Just three or four simple blooms can be tied with ribbon, labeled with each guest's name, and placed in a spare water glass at every setting.

left Gather cottage-garden flowers, such as sweet peas, roses, and viburnum, in soft, pastel tones. Lay extra glasses, like these pretty Moroccan tea glasses, at each place setting to keep the flowers fresh, ready to take home after the meal.
below Here, the dining-room windowsill is laden with blooms. The plants have been potted in simple pitchers and vases from the kitchen for a relaxed look to reflect the mood of the occasion.

A cymbidium orchid stem looks dramatic immersed in an over-sized glass vase. Change the water frequently and occasionally cut down the stem, and your orchid should last a long time.

Instead of opting for a traditional Christmas tree, try decorating cacti or other large indoor plants. Re-pot the plants in galvanized buckets and string them with festive lights.

Don't forget artificial flowers—they are particularly good value since they can be used time and time again, and are excellent for a lively party setting or a kitsch and colorful themed occasion. Pull the petals away from each flower head to scatter over the table, or simply float the complete head in a bowl.

The elements of lighting, flowers and plants can be put together very effectively. Float flower heads and petals together with floating candles in a large bowl on the table and try wrapping tree lights around potted plants. Place a thick candle in a storm lantern, wind light, or hurricane lamp, and stuff petals and flower heads around the sides to form a floral bed at the base of the candle. A string of electric lights wound around a tall potted cactus, cheese plant, or money plant will create an interesting light "sculpture," perfect for festive occasions, such as a modern-themed Christmas event or a New Year's Eve party.

An inexpensive option for flowers on the table is to fill a vase or dish with water and float colorful petals or flower heads. These chrysanthemum heads have been dyed with blue coloring and look wonderful floating among blue gel candles. This would make a perfect party table centerpiece—and talking point! Use variations of this idea to create areas of color and light on the table.

below Add slices of lime to the water in your ice-cube tray for drinks that are both refreshing and attractive.

right Traditional, practical glassware is always the best. This simple juicer is on hand for immediate fresh juice, which can be stored in an old glass milk bottle for breakfast time. The colored elements here are highlighted by the use of glass items.

opposite left Keep interesting packaging collected on your travels. These colorful tincans are useful for containing straws or knives and forks.

opposite right Interesting centerpieces can be built up from found objects. These shells were collected from the beach and strung together to wind around a tin plate laden with watermelon.

all the extras

Introduce any items that catch your eye and could serve as vessels for food, candles, or flowers. These often bring the most special touches to the table.

Often the most original and inventive pieces are found on a lazy Sunday morning wandering around a garage sale or spotted in the window of a local thrift store. You may be on vacation and happen to spy the most perfect soapstone bowl in a local craft shop or stroll along the beach and look down onto a cluster of interesting shells. All these items have their turn somewhere and will come out at the opportune moment—just remember that you have them and keep them close at hand.

Look for plates and dishes that can be used as centerpieces—interesting wooden or tin trays and bowls, or maybe a length of textured slate or cork to present condiments. Any pieces that can be used as storage vessels are worth considering for the table top, too—reuse tincans and jars for sugar, flatware, bread, flowers, and so on. It is all these little extras that give your setting an individual and unique edge, that your guests will appreciate and remember.

There are many festive occasions to inspire a special table setting, but sometimes it is just as enjoyable to make a celebration of a gathering with friends or a quiet evening in at home. The occasion or event can be your starting point for the theme of the table setting, such as eggs at Easter, or a traditional gold and red Christmas. Equally, inspiration can start with a bunch of favorite flowers, a special length of fabric that you'd like to use across the table, or some new floating candles to experiment with.

the occasions

right This sunny breakfast setting is enhanced by sticking to a palette of yellow and orange, with the strong spots of blue from the practical paper napkins.
below These colorful handmade egg cups are ideal for holding sea salt to pass around the breakfast table. You can also use egg cups for individual servings of butter and jelly at each setting.

weekday breakfast

For a weekday start, food needs to be fast, and you will want to offer family and guests a range of healthy options.

An early morning meal needs a setting that is practical, informal—and appealing enough to get out of bed for! Liven up the breakfast table with fresh, bold colors. Gather just a few colorful stems, such as ranuncula or large daisies, fresh from the yard. They will look great adorning the table, arranged simply in recycled bottles and jars, adding splashes of color to your table.

Clean, practical glassware looks good on the kitchen table and can be mixed and matched for an interesting setting. Be inventive with your use of simple kitchen items to serve food—use small plain glass pots to hold a choice of jelly or honey, and decant breakfast cereals into storage jars. A tin cup makes an interesting cornflake scoop, and colorful egg cups are just the right size for individual salt containers.

By carefully choosing the packaging of food elements, such as milk cartons and condiment pots, you can further stylize this type of setting. Use paper napkins and containers of ready-made yogurt

left Glass plates and bowls are both practical and stylish, and enhance the color scheme used on the table.
below Breakfast cereal has been decanted into this airtight storage jar so guests can see what they're getting! Scoop it out with a plain glass or a small cup.

to save time and dishwashing! Opt for individual glass jars of French yogurt (they can be reused later for homemade yogurt) and always have a jar of honey on hand.

A trolley laden with breakfast foods keeps the table top clear and can be wheeled between the eaters. You can use it to hold newspapers and magazines for easy access and to build up a collection of delicious jellies and honey for friends and family to take their pick. Just wipe the trolley off and tidy it up ready to wheel it out again the next morning. Bags of coffee, sugar, cereal, and bread can be resealed with colorful pegs, without the need to use plastic film or storage containers.

Stick to easy options for a weekday breakfast. That way, you will be able to enjoy your meal without feeling rushed.

right For a finishing touch, pop into the backyard and pick some fresh blooms. These glass milk bottles make interesting vases for single stems of ranuncula.
below Look for interesting food packaging that can be displayed on the table top. This Chinese honey pot looks great in this setting.

right Keep bags of fresh bread and cereals and packs of freshly ground coffee airtight by clipping with cheap-and-cheerful plastic pegs. This will keep them fresh and ready for latecomers to the breakfast table.

this page Individual jars of French yogurt look stylish at this breakfast spread. Keep the glass pots after the event and reuse them with homemade or decanted yogurt, or to hold candles at another occasion. Keep an abundance of paper napkins on hand and there will be no need for plates.

lazy weekend breakfast

Start the day with a wholesome breakfast over which family and friends can chat, relax, and plan the rest of the weekend.

A generous linen tablecloth provides an excellent base for a big breakfast. Throw it over a good-sized kitchen table and lay out enough china and flatware for your guests to indulge in whatever they fancy from your spread.

Start with basic but versatile china and accessories. The elements of a practical kitchen are ideal—plenty of uncomplicated glassware and simple, white china. Look for dual-purpose tableware, too: if you are serving boiled eggs, why not try reusing napkin rings as egg cups? And have fun with your settings. For example, personalize the boiled eggs before laying them out by simply jotting a guest's name on the shell in pencil. Or fill individual pots with butter, cool them, and write a name or initial with a skewer to mark each place. Make sure there is plenty of tea and coffee available—and don't fight over the newspapers!

opposite left Layer china at each setting with different-sized plates and top with a tall glass filled with yogurt and cereal.

opposite right Dig out individual glass jars for marmalade and pour fresh fruit juice into measuring cups. Dried apricots are excellent on cereal or just to nibble—and they match the color scheme, too!

left Bright flowers such as sunflowers or big daisies in tall jars are perfect for a sunny breakfast.

above Offer a choice of tea and coffee in labeled pots.

this page **The perfect setting for Sunday brunch! Aim to position your guests with a view out to the garden or at least by a window. That way they can check on what the weather is doing and make plans for the rest of the day.**

indulgent brunch

A table laid for a generous brunch is a perfect place to spend a long lazy Sunday, relaxing with your family and friends.

Choose a selection of plain white china and a full set of silverware or stainless steel flatware to give a clean fresh look to the table. Lay out an abundance of glassware to allow for plenty of water, juice, wine, and spicy Bloody Marys! A jar of mixed olives added to the line-up of glasses at each setting will provide something to nibble with a prebrunch drink while guests get comfortable. Finally, place cappuccino coffee cups and saucers at each setting, so everything is at hand and the coffee can be passed around the table.

Single stems of flowers work well at this style of setting. You want to give a splash of fresh color while still keeping the main body of the table top clear for the other elements. Cymbidium orchids are ideal. Though relatively expensive, a single stem goes a long way—and will look fresh for a long time.

left Each place setting is carefully labeled and laid out in the same way. Create order before the chaos ensues!
above Look for vases in interesting shapes and start building up a versatile collection.

opposite A placecard in the form of a luggage label has been carefully tied to this orchid flower.
left Here we see an individual setting in detail, with all the elements—the flatware, china, glassware, flower, and placecard—laid out neatly. Guests will each be handed a crisp linen napkin when they have taken their seats. The scattering of frosted-glass pebbles is a decorative touch against the harder lines of the overall setting.
below Fresh fruit preserves have been decanted into these airtight storage jars. Rest a teaspoon on top of each jar so guests can help themselves.

Pluck off the lower orchid heads complete with their short stems, place each in water in an individual jar (votive holders or shot glasses are ideal) and put one jar at each place setting. Luggage labels or price tickets can then be tied to each jar or stem to act as placecards—brunch is a good occasion to mix different groups of friends in an informal atmosphere. Keep the remaining orchid blooms on the longer stem for a taller plain-glass vase in the center of the table.

Lay the china, glassware, and flatware in a neat and formal way; then top each setting with something tasty, such as a bagel or muffin. The overall look of the setting should be orderly and stylish to avoid making the table look messy with all the different types of foods your guests will be eating. You can soften the hard shapes of the china and flatware with central clusters of decorative frosted-glass beads or pebbles. Once the food is put out, everything will be at hand, and guests and hosts can relax together.

shoreside picnic

Lay out a picnic on wooden decking overlooking a busy lake, where you can watch the fishing boats come in and out while indulging in a delicious waterside feast.

A more relaxed buffet-style spread is usually the best layout for this event. Let guests choose what they would like to eat and make sure there are plenty of napkins and flatware at hand.

Fold napkins—plain linen or squares of denim are ideal, but paper napkins are very convenient—and put them in separate bundles with a knife and fork. Tie each bundle with a small luggage label so guests can rummage for their own set.

Rather than adding herbs directly to a large salad, create a miniature, portable herb garden in a seed tray or large serving dish, so guests can help themselves to a fresh garnish. Ideal plants are parsley, rosemary, coriander, basil, mint, or chives. See what is available at the local supermarket or garden center.

Make sure there is plenty of fresh chilled spring water available. Prepare dishes of frozen fruit—slices of lime, lemon, and orange are great to flavor the water and keep it cool.

opposite left Be inventive with your containers for flatware and food. Why not use little metal buckets to hold knives and forks and save tincans for breadsticks and nuts, to fit in with the relaxed, outdoor feel?

opposite right Put a selection of three or four herb plants on a galvanized tray. Look after your portable garden, and it can be brought out again and again.

right Lay out the buffet elements across the ground. A large strip of raffia or a tablecloth folded lengthwise makes an excellent "base" for your picnic setting.

below When you are preparing food away from home, make good use of the natural objects like shells and stones you find around your picnic site.

Be inspired by your surroundings and incorporate natural elements from your picnic site into your table setting.

beach barbecue

Pack plenty of food and drink for a day at the beach. As the shadows start to lengthen, light the barbecue—and enjoy!

If you are planning a cookout at the beach, invest in a disposable barbecue—it is by far the easiest option. Surround it with large pebbles for decoration and added safety. If the meal is going to be a big event, with lots of hungry mouths to feed, a whole row of barbecues set up like this will look great.

Paper plates and napkins are the simplest option, as they can all be thrown into a big garbage bag at the end of the meal. Clip each plate together with a napkin and flatware, and supply tin cups as lightweight drinking vessels.

A plastic bucket can be used as a large cooler for food and drinks. Bring a bag of ice and let it slowly melt down in the bucket, or put the bucket firmly in the sand where the sea will lap around it and keep drinks cool. Make sure you pack plenty of storage jars filled with nuts, dried fruit, and other snacks to nibble on through the afternoon. They can be used when empty to transport leftover food home.

Finally, remember to take lanterns and big cozy blankets for when the sun goes down. Bring out vacuum flasks of warming soup to pass around, and there will be no need to hurry home.

opposite A barbecue on the beach—what a treat! Make sure you take everything you need so you are set up for the day. Disposable paper plates and napkins are a must. A big beach blanket, a radio, and lots of reading matter are necessities, and take a few lanterns to find your way back through the dunes in the dark!

below A napkin, a straw, a fork, and a paper plate are all held together with a useful wooden clothespin to give as a complete bundle to each guest.

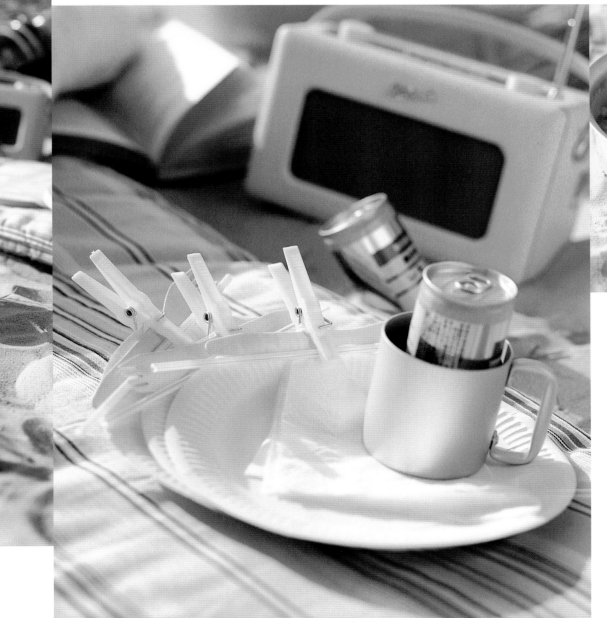

top Breadsticks are tied in a bundle with string, and a denim dishtowel has been rolled up and secured with a length of twine and a shell.

above A large aluminum bowl makes a practical carrier for food and can be used as a drinks chiller once you arrive at your picnic spot.

mediterranean-style table

Prepare an alfresco lunch on the terrace, combining deep blue with white and accents of bright bougainvillea—for a look evoking summer vacations spent beside the Mediterranean.

You don't need a large backyard for open-air dining. Any outdoor space will do, as long as there is enough room for a table! Whitewashed wood and old outdoor furniture are ideal surfaces to build up a Mediterranean-themed setting, but any table will do. Try a sturdy carpenter's table if you don't have any outdoor furniture, and cover it with a large cloth.

Stick to a color scheme of Mediterranean tones, using white, bright pink, and sea blue. The best table elements for this theme are chunky glassware, preferably

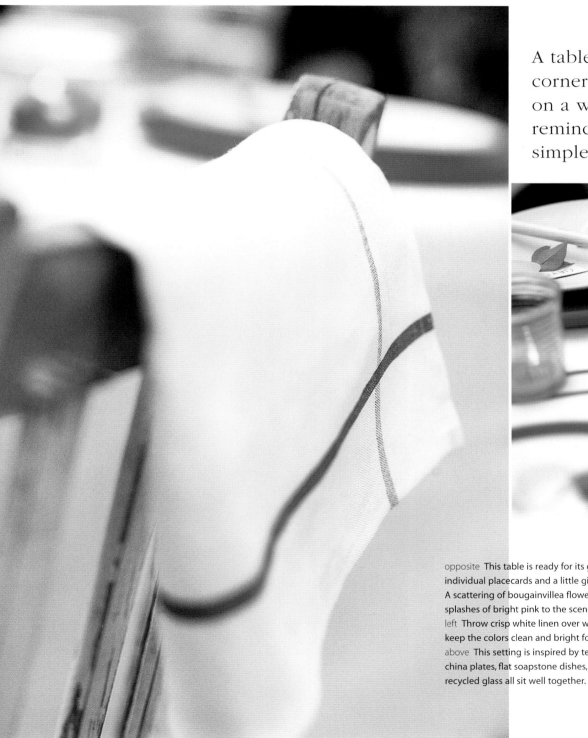

A table laid in a shady corner of the backyard on a warm afternoon reminds us of life's simple pleasures.

opposite This table is ready for its guests. All the settings have individual placecards and a little gift in a bouquet garni bag. A scattering of bougainvillea flower heads adds decorative splashes of bright pink to the scene.

left Throw crisp white linen over weathered wooden chairs, and keep the colors clean and bright for an informal outdoor meal.

above This setting is inspired by texture as well as color. Heavy china plates, flat soapstone dishes, wooden soup spoons, and recycled glass all sit well together.

above This deep-blue colored china works well in a Mediterranean-inspired table setting and will sit happily on top of plain white china plates for a more informal family meal. The blue-and-white checked dishtowel is a necessary part of the well-equipped kitchen and can double as table linen for this setting.

right Dangle lanterns from any available branch or wall. The version shown here is big enough to hold a larger candle that will stay lit for hours. Make your own lanterns from discarded glass jars—just wash thoroughly, remove the labels, and hang them in groups around your Mediterranean setting.

Whatever the occasion, have fun with the table by putting extra thought into the presentation and the surrounding environment.

the thick, recycled variety, and a mixture of china in soapstone and matt ceramic. If you have any blue pieces, mix them with white china and stick to plain white candles.

If your outdoor space is lacking in color and foliage, invest in colorful additions, such as bougainvillea, or bring out house plants for the day to liven up the scene. Repot them in aluminum buckets, galvanized containers, and large terracotta pots to create your Mediterranean environment, and remove loose petals to scatter over the table. Any old buckets that aren't full of flowers can be used to hold pebbles or floating candles, so your theme is taken beyond the table top.

Even if it is daylight when you begin to eat, it is always special to have candles on the table, and it means that guests can sit around until the light goes down. Lanterns are fun, too, and perfect to make sure candles stay alight in the breeze when dining outdoors. They can be hung from surrounding branches and fencing. Choose smaller jars for little candles and be inventive with what the candles are in. White sand, gravel, or the course salt used in dishwashers are ideal. Look for chips of colored mosaic glass— often found in florists and craft stores. Pet stores and aquatic suppliers stock colored sand in shades of pink and blue that are also suitable for a Mediterranean-style table.

right A miniature cacti garden makes an unusual and fitting "centerpiece." Tiny pots of cacti have been set in a bed of white gravel scattered with glass mosaic.
below Chips of colored glass mosaic have been put in the base of candleholders to spread color across the table.

A fresh, modern approach to decorating the table will
make for happy guests and encourage good conversation.

modern chic dining

With a little inspiration, and a minimum of fuss, you can turn a simple meal with friends into a really special occasion.

At this sort of gathering, seat guests at the ends of the table as well as along the sides, so everyone can scan the table as a whole. Lay each place setting with a basic knife, fork, and spoon and a large platter, then play around with china and use cups and saucers for dessert. Instead of using a tablecloth, keep things simple by laying each setting on an individual placemat.

Steel and aluminum will sit well with this contemporary look. Search for little metal cases for candles or put votive candles in pie plates, and use seed trays or a planter for the centerpiece. Vegetables can be as attractive as fruit or flowers on the table, and succulents will fit well in this environment, so try piling the central planter with interesting shapes, such as squash or artichoke heads—they can be cooked for dinner the next day!

Raw materials like slate will also complement this minimal setting. Slate placemats are widely available and can double as chalkboards. You could put a piece at each place setting and write

opposite and left **Stick to a neutral color scheme—natural earthenware, plain-styled flatware and clear, simple glassware complement raw materials like wood and slate.**
below **Use the slate placemats to start a table game between courses.**

this page **This cool modern table setting is perfect for a lunchtime gathering. Settings are marked neatly with placemats, and a large versatile platter at each setting holds a napkin and napkin ring. A centerpiece of large artichoke heads makes an unusual but stylish impact. A bowl of fruit would also have worked well here—guests could then have helped themselves for dessert.**

Pale wood, white Formica, and cool shades of green all work toward the light, airy feel.

out your guests' names, or simply use the slate for games. A less expensive alternative that will work just as well is to buy chopping boards or squares of plywood and paint them with blackboard paint.

Keep glassware simple, but be inventive with placecards. Cards can be spiked on bamboo skewers or cocktail sticks to indicate seating arrangements.

A perfect setting for this meal is a minimal dining room or a large modern stainless-steel kitchen, but don't feel restricted by your environment. Simply clear away as much clutter from the room as possible for a fresh, contemporary feel, or adapt the table decoration to take in inspiration from the rest of the room. Sticking to a neutral palette with shades of gray and green will keep this setting fresh and relaxed, while the odd floating candle and pairs of glowing votives dotted over the table top remind guests that it is a special occasion.

above Floating candles gently illuminate the corners of the table and introduce the element of water to the setting. They have been layered by placing the bowls on small linen coasters to coordinate with the placemats. A bamboo skewer becomes an inventive placecard spike, and a handy piece of lime sits below for both decoration and practicality.

above left A piece of slate becomes a useful condiment tray. The oil and vinegar have been decanted into recycled glass jars and can be poured back after the meal or resealed for later.

asian-style banquet

Don't worry if you don't have a dining table; a low surface, such as a coffee table,
is an excellent starting point for an oriental-inspired meal. Search your home for
pillows and cushions to scatter on the floor around the table for low-level seating.

Eating at a low-level dining area, seated on silk pillows, will give you a really decadent, oriental feel. If you make your own pillows, buy enough material for a matching panel at the window.

Simple heavy linen or a long raffia mat over the table top will provide a good base on which to build. Choose simple shapes in basic neutral colors and add splashes of bright color with suitable flowers—magenta-colored Singapore orchids are ideal here, and once again you can economize by plucking lower flower heads to float singly. Pale duck-egg blue and sage green will also go well with this muted palette. Pull up a nearby bench to stack any extra china necessary for the following courses—this will help keep the table top clear and uncomplicated.

Have a good look around an oriental food store for individual bottles of drink to put in place of glasses at each setting. There are fun packages of fruit juice to be found, and little bottles of saki will also work well. Individual glass bottles can also be effectively reused for flowers or chilled water at another occasion. Try lining up a multiple row of bottles along the length of the table and pop a single stem of decorative grass in each.

opposite top Create a "centerpiece" from a large dish or tray holding unusual dishes and bottles of soy sauce and oil so guests can help themselves.
below left and opposite main The strong graphic lines characteristic of an Asian theme are relaxed with the addition of small pots and bowls for flowers, candles, and seeds.
below Stick to the basics—a noodle bowl, napkin, and chopsticks—at each place.

lunch on the lawn

Taking your lunch out into the yard is always a special treat. Here, even the simplest of salads deserves a well-considered setting.

Soften the look of a metal table with a loosely woven piece of plain linen. It will blow in the breeze for a fresh, floaty, romantic look, perfect for a bright summer's day lunch, and will work equally well for a balmy early evening supper.

Keep the color scheme simple and uncomplicated, using neutrals and shades of white. Natural elements, such as soapstone, raw linen, and dried flower heads, will fit in well with the setting. Take inspiration from your surroundings for colors and materials, using delicately colored flowers on the table and grasses, such as bear grass and snake grass, to tie around rolled napkins or glasses.

A plain altar candle will provide a simple centerpiece, and an ice-filled vase makes a cooling water-bottle holder. Lay each place setting with a simple large dish and a single fork to enjoy a

A couple of soft pink garden blooms add spots of color to this understated alfresco dining area, without competing with the colors of the summer garden all around. The flowers sit in simple tall glass jars or clear-glass water bottles, and decorative butterflies perch on the edge of each wineglass.

Make the most of a breezy, summer afternoon by
carrying a table onto the lawn and serving a crisp salad.

summer salad. Fold plain linen napkins down to coaster size and place them under water glasses. Feel inspired to mix cooling summer drinks. Cut up tiny cubes of lemon and lime and add them to your ice-cube tray when you fill it. These will look and taste fabulous in a glass of sparkling spring water.

Linen is the perfect fabric for a tablecloth and napkins at this event. A bleached denim would look equally good outside, especially if an ugly table has to be hidden away. Plain unbleached cotton voile fabric is also an inexpensive way to cover an alfresco table.

Soapstone looks good in a natural, neutral setting, but bleached wooden bowls would work equally well, and remember those glass plates if you need to lay your hands on extra pieces that won't dominate the general ambience of the table top. Choose thick chunky glass, preferably recycled, and, if you can't decant your drinks, stick to sympathetic spring-water packaging, since these bottles are sometimes made from recycled glass themselves, with attractive labels.

Hang simple lanterns made from recycled glass jars from surrounding branches so your meal can last into dusk.

above left **This table is very simply laid, with lots of natural elements, such as loosely woven raw linen, soapstone platters, and recycled glass. The soapstone glasses and vase (which is used here to hold the water bottle) have practical value, too, as the stone's insulating properties will keep cold drinks cool on a hot afternoon.**

opposite right Each place has its own little dish of sea salt and
coarsely ground black pepper to sprinkle over the salad if desired.
A dried flower head is a delicate addition to the setting.
this page A strand of bear grass has been carefully tied around the
cup for a decorative touch. A plain linen napkin is presented in a
new way, by folding it and putting it beneath the beaker.

eastern-style elegance

Be experimental with color for an elegant, Asian-themed dinner party. It's fun to mix strong colors together on the table top.

Colored cut glass works well within this theme. Scour antique stores and markets for interesting pieces. Don't worry if you only manage to find single glasses; they can be used as unusual votive holders or mixed with other odd pieces for a more bohemian look. Find a sumptuous piece of fabric to use as a runner or tablecloth, and choose napkins that will work well with it. Experiment with folding them in different ways, and, for a change, try placing them under the plates.

Place a row of plants along the center of the table lengthwise. If possible, re-plant them in bowls that match the dinner set you are using. Orchids are ideal for an Asian theme: their roots are reasonably shallow, and the plants can be easily transferred and reused in other table settings. Try to pick plants with a deep color to their flowers that mixes well with the other colored table elements.

opposite left   Mix materials around the table. Silver cups reflect surrounding colors for an interesting surface effect that brings everything together visually.

opposite right   The thin stem of an orchid is perfect for a table situation, where guests won't want to peer at each other through bushy plants.

above   Be decorative with foliage, too—an interesting leaf will give texture to a side plate—but be sure to avoid any poisonous varieties!

right   Draw inspiration from fabrics and furnishings around your home. A length of unusual fabric makes a great runner. Pick out colors from it to reflect in your choice of elements.

cool classic dining

A formal occasion calls for an elegant
table with lots of crisp white linen,
fine china, and sparkling glassware.

It's always a pleasure to have the chance to
do something special with table settings,
and a formal dinner gives you the perfect
opportunity. If you are using an everyday
dining surface, opt for a starched white
tablecloth or placemats. If you have neither
of these, why not use well-ironed clean
white napkins to mark each place at the
table? If the napkins cover more than
the width of the table when they are placed
opposite each other, think of each pair as a
runner across the surface and allow them
to overhang the edges of the table.

Flowers and foliage can be most
effective when they are kept to a minimum.
Here, the odd frond of fern in a simple
vase will be just enough to accentuate the
clean, starched look. Carefully consider
shapes at this table, and choose vases that
won't detract from the setting as a whole. A
low, round vase is ideal, as is a spherical
fishbowl shape. If you are short of vases,

right **A beaded napkin ring is a decadent placecard
holder, and gel candles mix well with fine glassware.**
opposite **Warm candlelight gives a magical glow that
extends over the mantelpiece and sideboard,
combining with the soft fern fronds to bring subtle
elegance to the occasion.**

Choose classic simple shapes for stylish elegance
and keep everything to a minimum.

substitute a plain clear bottle or a clean decanter. Pick out the green of the foliage with fresh fruit that can be served after the meal—pears and green apples will always fit into an elegant setting and sit decoratively in a stemmed dish or plain white ceramic fruit bowl.

Keep the atmosphere clean but moody with lots of little table candles. Plain metal-cased votives are ideal and can be set in neat lines around the table. Look for small plain-glass votive holders, too, that will add to the minimal feel. Invest in some glass droplets or larger hollow balls (available from florists and gift shops) to sit between the candles or in clusters in glass bowls. The abundance of clean, clear glass will give your table ultimate elegance.

By using simple elements and minimal colors, you will accentuate the shapes laid out on the table top. Play around with this idea, and try to offset the circular shapes of china and glassware with harder lines of flatware and linen. As long as the elements involved in this elegant setting are uniform, they needn't be expensive. It is the clean lines and overall orderliness of the presentation that will give it a stylish look.

left Pairs of well-starched linen placemats have been joined together to lie across the table and gently drape over each side. A matching napkin sits along the back of each chair.
opposite main Between the lines of white linen, rows of hollow glass balls have been interspersed with votives, accentuating the glowing spots of light.

below A plain-glass dip tray found in a thrift store makes an excellent dish for nibbles.

bottom left This is a very graphic setting, with lots of circular objects set out in orderly lines. The minimal fern fronds give it a hint of softness; cool white calla lilies would have fitted in well here, too.

exotic finger-food feast

Go to town with color and prepare for an exotic-styled meal. Set a low table with rich fabrics and scatter plenty of comfortable pillows for guests to sit on.

Think of exotic, far-flung lands and feel inspired. Gather up plenty of different-sized pillows from around the house and make simple covers for them from bright satin fabric—lining fabric works well, too, and can be found at reasonable prices. Make sure there's plenty of leftover fabric to be used to make a set of napkins and a table runner in coordinating colors.

Exotic flowers are ideally suited to this occasion, but colorful gerbera and carnations will look just as good and cost far less. Float the flower heads in small colored bowls dotted around the table top. Clean glass votive holders or Moroccan tea glasses make perfect drinking glasses for wine and fruit juice. Decant colored liquids into interesting vessels and empty bottles. Why not try adding a drop of grenadine or colored fruit cordial to spring water for a special exotic-looking drink?

Don't worry too much about the practicality of eating a full meal at this type of setting. Offer a selection of bread in a dark wooden bowl or marble dish, provide lots of finger food … and make sure there are plenty of napkins on hand!

left Use candles and tree lights to illuminate your dining area. Be inventive: a bright sheet or scarf makes an excellent tablecloth. And try putting tree lights under a glass-topped table to create an interesting glow through your tablecloth.
below Cut up slices of exotic fruit to offer to your guests and to decorate the table top. Guests will have fun testing and sharing new flavors.

this page, main Low-hanging lights, such as colored glass Indian and Moroccan lanterns, add to the warmth and intimacy of the occasion and are easily illuminated with single votive candles.
this page, inset Tiny colored glass bowls hold floating flower heads in bright hues. These look very exotic against the richly colored pashmina that has been used to cover the table.

romantic meal for two

Plan ahead and get everything ready in advance, so you can unplug the phone, relax, and enjoy each other's undivided attention.

A special romantic table setting is suitable for all sorts of occasions. Obvious opportunities are Valentine's Day or an anniversary, but this is also an enjoyable table to set up for a quiet birthday meal or to celebrate a promotion at work. Or why not just celebrate being romantic?

Red is a good—and traditional—color for romantic liaisons and can look stunning mixed with everyday glassware. Choose modern functional table elements to brighten up the setting, and use plain red napkins—fabric or paper, depending on the formality of the occasion. Simple square napkins can be easily made at home from red cotton fabric, but paper napkins often add an interesting twist to an indoor meal.

Decorate the table top with little gifts that fit in with the occasion. Find photographs to remind you both of special times. Miniature chocolates are a nice

above left The look needn't be dark and heavy to create an intimate setting. This bright studio apartment dresses up well for a romantic meal. The color red has been spread around the room—and is even extended to the windowboxes! Red and green work particularly well together and here are accentuated in the choice of elements—the glassware, china, and flowers—all perfectly set off against the simple glass table top.
above A collection of candles has been grouped together, displayed in a variety of votive holders and everyday glasses to match the red-and-green color scheme. They will all be lit as the evening grows darker.

left Try layering plain glass plates with colored china and choose flatware with colored handles or use bright chopsticks. Chopsticks can be bought in a variety of colors or you can paint them yourself, using nontoxic paint.

below Collect votive holders in clean bright colors and recycle them as individual salt and pepper holders.

this page The table has been decorated with a mixture of carefully picked items. Miniature twinkling tree lights are intertwined around spiky grass plants. Sticks with a display of bright-red feathers were found at a local florist and can be used to stir cocktails. A strand of bear grass ties the chopsticks together, and a fig sits on a carefully layered stack of china and glass.

Any day can become a romantic occasion …
make the most of your time together.

surprise, as are individual bottles of brightly colored drink, such as Campari. Drink cranberry juice or add grenadine to wine or sparking water for more color, and choose exotic fruit, such as figs or dates, as an attractive starter.

Another chance to bring color and texture to the table is to tie flatware or chopsticks together. Use thick strands of grass or clusters of feathers with a wired malleable end and keep a collection of beads or buttons to tie around glassware.

Cacti and grasses will look interesting and unusual at this setting—that is, if you're not opting for red roses! Use plain-glass mixing bowls for pots and put the plants on beds of white gravel or stones. Miniature tree lights are relatively easy to come by and can be twisted into potted plants to jazz up the table lighting. If the table is by a window, extend your inspiration to colorful windowboxes, to blend the setting in with the rest of the room.

above left A card-holder is a fun way to present placecards. Dig out old photographs of the two of you and share happy memories. above Glassware can be basic and is made decorative with the simple addition of a colored plastic heart attached with thin jewelry wire. Miniature bottles of drinks are a special touch at each place setting. Aim to color-coordinate these, too.

above The clean modern lines of this classic glass table and leather chairs make a great base to build a Father's Day spread. Colors have been kept reasonably masculine, with dark stoneware and gray felt placemats and coasters. The yellow glassware makes an interesting combination.

father's day spread

Father's Day offers an opportunity to present a more masculine style of setting, which would also be suitable for a formal occasion, such as a business lunch.

Aim to set the table in a stylish way, led by your father's favorite colors. Heavy dark china will sit well with colorful glassware and give a modern look to the setting.

A glass-topped table is an excellent base to show off these different textures and colors. Felt is also an interesting surface to work on and can be easily cut to the shape of the table top if you want to disguise it—dark brown or gray are good colors to opt for. A simple linen runner will soften and protect a glass table—if you are making your own, why not combine two colors so you have different-colored ends, and make matching napkins in alternate colors? For a set of four napkins, choose two colors and make two napkins predominantly one color with a coordinating stripe; and vice versa for the second pair.

Protect your table top with mats and coasters. Leather, fleece, and felt are all good materials to cut up into simple shapes. Add interest by using pinking shears around the edges or cut central holes or initials into the mats.

main A bundle of bamboo stalks tied with a strand of bear grass decorates each place setting. The drinking glasses have been placed upside down for a change, and a little prewrapped pack of crackers is laid to the right of the setting for each guest.
above right A plain-glass votive holder has been wrapped with a piece of oriental paper to give an interesting glow.
above far right A square tank vase makes an ideal deep vessel for a selection of olives. Sit them stylishly on pieces of banana leaf.

Fine glassware sits with heavy china for a masculine feel. The glass table top means that all colors are seen clearly.

"Lay" plates give a chic, ordered look to the table and are useful for resting bread and flatware. The flatware should be stylish and simple, sticking to the minimum number of utensils needed on the table.

Individual salt shakers are fun, and placecards sit well in the collection of elements at each place. Add predinner nibbles at each setting, too, in the form of decorative table treats. Scour oriental supermarkets for chips or crackers in interesting packaging.

Experiment with ways of presenting glassware—

stack pieces, lay them upside down, and mix different sizes of glasses. Wrapping simple glass votive holders will add interest to the table lighting. Chinese and Japanese paper are ideal, and tissue and crepe paper also work well. Combine these with floating candles in circular dishes or interesting ashtrays.

Choose minimal stems, such as apple blossom, pussy willow, and bamboo, to stand in vases on the table and surrounding areas. They will last for a long time and don't need much looking after.

above A placecard nestles in each bowl alongside an interesting salt shaker. The white china looks great against the darker stoneware.
above left Decant red wine into a plain glass decanter, put it among the other metal- and glassware, and watch all the reflections work together on the table top.

All the colors on this table work extremely well together. Don't be afraid of using dark shades—as long as the setting is lightened with the occasional piece of bright glassware. The oriental paper with gold-leaf decoration that has been wrapped around the votive holders gives a special glow that also livens up the surrounding glass elements.

Flowers are a good starting point for a Mother's Day setting. Pick out soft pastel shades of color inspired by seasonal sweet peas, peonies, and pansies.

mother's day treat

A Mother's Day lunch is a good opportunity to bring out special pieces of china and glassware. Dainty glass plates and softly toned drinking glasses look elegant laid out on a special tablecloth. Mix and match them at each place setting and use them to display cakes, sandwiches, fruit, candy, and flowers on the table top. Silver or clear acrylic-handled flatware will also work well in this setting. And select napkins in different shades from the same palette.

Don't be afraid to mix different colors and styles of glassware, linen, and silverware. So long as you stick to the same soft color palette and don't overload the table, it will all look good together. By using more glassware, you will pick up subtle colors and keep the table looking fresh. Large apothecary jars look great with pastel-colored after-dinner bonbons or simply filled with crumpled tissue paper to bring more areas of color to the table top and surrounding surfaces.

opposite and left **The pastel colors of the flowers and table linen, along with the dainty pieces of glassware, make this an excellent setting for a Mother's Day lunch.** below **For a pretty display, float hollow glass beads in a glass bowl among softly colored petals and flower heads.**

Choose her favorite flower for the theme of the whole table setting.

Look for prettily packaged cakes and cookies for this Mother's Day treat. Scour your local delicatessen for unusual desserts and place them on a fine glass platter or special china plate on the center of the table top to be lit by a ring of pretty votive candles in clear glass holders. It needn't be expensive to look good in this setting!

Be inventive with flowers. Put the table near an open window, where you can enjoy natural light, and extend your pretty color scheme around the room and beyond, with flowers on the mantelpiece and windowsill, and tiny jars of candles hanging from bright ribbon. Cottage-garden flowers are ideal for this occasion and can be displayed in lots of ways. Re-plant pansies in recycled pitchers and vases to decorate the area around the table. Pull petals from sweet peas and other delicate flowers to float in glass vases and continue the colors around the room. A single carnation head holds a wealth of petals that can be separated and floated in glass bowls of water.

Everyone appreciates a table gift, so indulge your guests with their own flowers at each setting. Choose pretty glasses to stand them in after tying with ribbon, so guests can take them away after the meal.

left Good-quality silverware is laid out next to a pretty bobble-edged plate all ready for a Mother's Day tea. Each place setting has its own miniature flower bouquet for the guests to take away with them. Softly colored glasses and patterned Moroccan tea glasses enhance the scheme, while a carefully chosen prepackaged bottle of green tea sits happily among the decor.

top A miniature glass lantern hangs from a length of pink ribbon
at the window next to the table.
above The beautifully packaged Italian dessert sits decoratively
inside a ring of dainty glowing gel candles set out on a glass platter.
right An old wine bottle with a particularly attractive label makes
an ideal vase for a full-headed peony. Put it on the mantelpiece
beside a large mirror and you get two displays!

baby shower tea

Set an informal table in soft, pastel tones. The overall look will be pretty and peaceful—perfect to celebrate the imminent arrival of a new baby.

A baby shower is a very special occasion among friends and family, and is a wonderful excuse for a gathering. If you have a large kitchen table, make it the main base for the occasion, and guests can roam around the rest of the house if they desire. If you are expecting a lot of visitors, lay a themed buffet table; if you are having a smaller party, stick to a simpler table layout.

Pale pink and blue are obvious colors for this event and will work well in a kitchen environment. If you have a solid wooden table, expose the bare wood and lay a series of runners across the width. Alternatively, lay the runners over a crisp white tablecloth. Cotton gingham is inexpensive and will look fresh and stylish on the table top. If you are making table runners yourself, you won't need much fabric for it to have an impact. Three pieces of gingham that just hang over

opposite left Pink gingham table runners provide a good base for this orderly setting. Cotton coasters and square glass candleholders sit alternately along the center of the table and echo the geometric print of the runners underneath.
opposite right Practical and basic, French glasses make great containers for sugar and candy, and match the chosen color scheme!
left Try using small bottle vases of different shapes together and place them in a line to contain similar-colored displays of flowers.
below A pink candle sits in a bed of dishwasher salt.

opposite **Place the runners widthwise across the table and aim to arrange pairs of place settings opposite each other.**
left These special flowers have been carefully chosen for their color and are tied together with grass—a collection of such arrangements makes an unusual and eye-catching display.
above A length of pink gingham ribbon carefully tied around each homemade napkin gives the perfect finishing touch.

opposite edges will suffice. Set up places opposite each other on the runners; the symmetry will fit well with the geometric fabric pattern. It's also fun to mix different sizes of gingham print, but try not to become too complicated—stick to either pink-and-white or blue-and-white checks. Napkins can be sewn from gingham or from plain pieces of cotton, which are then tied with gingham ribbon or strips of fabric left over from making the runners.

If you have any pastel-colored china, now is the chance to use it. Basic everyday white china will also look good, as will practical glassware—look for heavy French tumblers and anything tinted slightly with the colors you have chosen.

Pale pink and white candy and marshmallows are decorative and make excellent nibbles (for adults and children alike). Put them in glasses and display them in a row along the center of the table between glasses of water.

For pretty flower displays, mix individual stems such as miniature roses, lizianthus, and eucalyptus, and use grasses to tie flowers together creatively.

children's party

Think bright and cheerful. Blow up a few balloons to trigger your inspiration for the party—this is one occasion when you can let your imagination run wild!

The kitchen is an ideal setting for a fun children's party. Here spillages don't matter too much, and everything is on hand for serving food and clearing up. It is always good to have outdoor access, too, so party games can overflow into the yard.

The elements you employ needn't be expensive. Peel the labels off clear plastic bottles and fill them with colorful drinks to help the effect—the way the food and drink looks is just as important as the way it tastes! Make placemats from craft felt, or cut squares of bright carpet remnants or astroturf for a surreal effect kids will love.

Place a practical glass or metal bowl at each place setting (a basic mixing bowl will do) and pile it with goodies: a lunch box to eat from and pieces of dried fruit and other treats wrapped in plain-colored paper tied with string. This will make the meal seem "gift-like" for all concerned!

right Tree lights adorned with artificial flowers will liven up the table and surrounding areas, and are an especially good idea if you want to avoid using candles. A string of lights placed along the length of the table should give enough illumination without encroaching on individual settings.

Stick to a palette of bright primary colors for maximum "wow" factor.

below To make sure all your guests take their seats, personalize each setting with imaginative placecards that children will really appreciate—here, Polaroid photographs were taken in the yard beforehand and then clipped to each bowl.
right Toy goldfish swimming in a large plastic bowl make an irresistible centerpiece.

above If you want to protect the table surface, invest in a paper tablecloth and be sure to leave out lots of crayons to draw with. Paper tablecloths are available in a wide range of bright colors, which are bound to inspire little artists!

opposite Brightly colored parrots sit on the back of each chair to welcome their guest! Each place setting is busy with colorful ideas to eat, drink, and play with—perfect to entice young partygoers.

Prepare clear plastic dishes of fruit gelatin in lots of different colors for dessert and decorate the table with all the right party animals—rubber frogs, artificial goldfish, and colorful toy parrots perched on the backs of the chairs.

Think of unusual party gifts for guests to take away. A miniature cactus at each setting will be fun and low-maintenance, but take care to plant them so that grabbing hands are safe from prickles. Foil takeout food containers or small boxes and bags can be personalized and filled with more goodies.

This is an opportunity to be as inventive as possible with your table setting. Just remember to stick to a bright color palette and incorporate as many quirky pieces onto the table as you can. Clip, float, pot, and place objects to keep your little guests happy and occupied throughout the party meal.

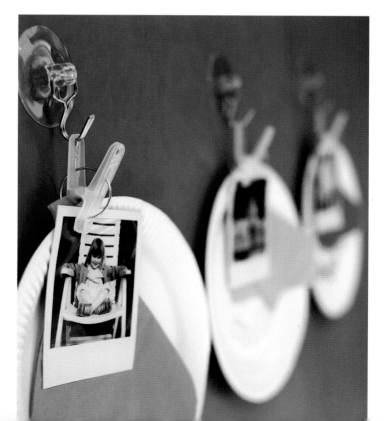

top Display bright flowers, such as gerbera, in plastic water bottles for fun.
above A blue frog, a potted cactus, a bowl of jello, a square of grass, and a host of irresistible packages—turn the table into a wonderland!
left Hang personalized paper plates and napkins along the wall, ready to be grabbed when the birthday cake comes out.

surprise birthday buffet

Buffets are ideal for parties. Choose the guest of honor's favorite color as inspiration, and stick to it for everything you use—even the food!

A basic table or sideboard makes a good buffet surface. You could lay everything out over a stretch of kitchen work surface, but a freestanding table is the best option. Why not invest in a basic wallpaper-pasting table for this sort of event— then it can be easily be folded away and stored ready for the next occasion?

Decorate the area surrounding your buffet table in the same color scheme. Hang decorations or paper lanterns above the table from a piece of ribbon suspended from each side of the room. Exploit your color scheme further and

Choose your dominant color, make your second color white, and add clear glassware for maximum vibrancy on the table top.

opposite Everything here has been arranged in groups for the guests to choose from. Clear-glass tank vases are excellent to hold both food and decorations. Candles in a central vase can be lit as the party goes on into the evening. A small bunch of carnations makes a pretty token leaving gift.

left Single birthday candles have been placed in individual meringues so everyone gets a birthday wish!

above A line of bright-pink vodka gelatines sits temptingly along the window ledge. Floral-decorated tree lights add a practical and fun touch to the setting—keep them on all day for spots of light.

this page, inset A line of Chinese paper lanterns accentuates the dominant color choice at this party. Anything works, as long as it fits in with the scheme: a bright-pink bucket makes an ideal home for an orchid; and cartons of guava juice were chosen for their garish packaging. A length of wallpaper makes an interesting and practical table covering and sheets of vibrant paper add to the total layout.
this page, main Ricepaper flowers found in an oriental supermarket make a pretty buffet offering.

make coordinating gelatine—vodka jello if your guests are old enough! Choose candy, candles, cookies, and paper plates to fit the scene and rummage around for extra decorative touches, such as feathers and artificial flowers.

Instead of overloading a single cake with birthday candles, plant them in individual meringues or cupcakes. If you are doing the baking yourself, remember the power of food coloring—a blue cake can be most alluring in the right setting! Decorate everyday glassware and plastic cups to fit in with your setting. Why not try stickers or use transfers? An extra-special and inexpensive idea is to prepare colored ice cubes or, for a more subtle touch, add bright edible flower petals to your ice cube tray.

Candles of all shapes and sizes can be used at this event. You can stand candles in jars and tanks of sand or dishwasher salt if you do not have enough candlesticks—this looks effective with different shades of the same color bunched up together. Tree lights are a good choice for a birthday buffet, too. Hang them in clusters around the room, occasionally adding artificial flowers or rosettes of tissue paper to the cord (well away from the bulbs) to dress them in true party spirit!

above right **This stemmed bowl holds party bags for each guest to take home with them. Make little gift bags for guests and fill them with special foil-wrapped chocolates or tiny gifts, such as pieces of jewelry. Pins or clips are ideal to seal the bags; decorate them with feathers and self-adhesive "jewels."**
right **This large votive candle sits inside a group of bangles for decoration. Votives make inexpensive party lighting. Place them in groups around the room and decorate the metal cases with metallic ribbon or glitter.**

Falling on a Sunday, Easter is a good day for a special lunch with family and friends. It also provides another great opportunity for themed table settings.

easter celebration

A palette of soft pastels lends itself well to this occasion. Work toward feminine shades of pale pink, green, and blue, and introduce a layered theme with table linen. Textured natural linen is the ideal fabric for a table runner. If you want to make your own runner, buy a length of fabric long enough to drape slightly over the table ends and cut a suitable width. Hem along both long sides and gently fringe the shorter edges. Use any spare fabric for matching napkins.

If you are having lots of guests and setting a large table, there's no need to own a complete set of matching china. Try mixing different-patterned china in similar colors. Pile plates together, starting with the dinner plate, then a smaller plate, and top with a dish or bowl for the appetizer. And, for a festive centerpiece, buy some tester pots of chalky pastel-colored flat latex paint and decorate eggs to sit in small bowls and tall egg cups.

above The plates have been laid alternately in stripes and dots so no two settings opposite or alongside each other are the same.
right These eggs have been blown and painted in pastel shades to sit on a bed of silk and feathers as a decorative table piece.

this page **This table has been placed in the living room to be by the French doors leading outdoors for a quick egg-hunt-getaway after the meal! The surrounding areas—the side table and sofa—have also been decorated in the same color scheme. Simple pillows made from plain raw silk add areas of brighter color within the dreamy scheme.**

above For extra decoration at each setting, make individual "nests" from rings of feathers to enclose ceramic or hard-boiled eggs.

above right Choose blooms in soft pink and lilac—peonies are ideal and pale-pink carnations will always look good. Carry the decorative theme through to the flowers by adding elements from the table, such as sticks with feathers tied to their tips.

Touches of hot pink will liven up the pastel color scheme. Look for lengths of pink ribbon and bright silk pillows to dot around to create more of a comfortable and informal setting suited to a family meal. Cushion covers in interesting textures can also be used as temporary seat covers.

This is a good opportunity to play with textures, incorporating chalky eggshells and delicate soft feathers. Everyone enjoys a festive occasion, so carry on the theme within individual settings, laying "nests" for each guest and providing them with chocolate eggs to be getting on with before the main meal is served.

The combination of the airy linen tablecloth and pastel china and eggs gives an overall delicate and feminine feel to this occasion. And the humorous touches of fluffy feathers and chocolate eggs will appeal to guests young and old.

Place the table by a large window or French doors overlooking the yard to view any prospective after-lunch egg hunts.

above Take inspiration from the occasion and incorporate feathers into the table setting. Table gifts are very fitting to a festive meal—try making individual "nests" from plain-glass votive holders and use double-sided tape to attach pure white feathers around the sides.

left Instead of formal placecards, use pretty ribbon to tie an old-fashioned luggage label to the back of each chair.

rustic thanksgiving

Try something a little different for Thanksgiving dinner, and decorate a humble kitchen table with the fruits and colors of the season.

Get inspired by the colors of the fall—mustard, amber, orange, red, deep green—and create a setting for a simple Thanksgiving family meal. It's fun to have lots of relevant vegetation adorning the table for this themed occasion: gourds, artichokes, oranges, and satsumas all work well together.

Enjoy the textures of the fruit and vegetables, and try to reflect this in your selection of elements. If you have thick ceramic bowls and plates in different colors, now is the time to bring them out. Aim to unify the spread by sitting each bowl upon a "lay" plate—wood or rattan is ideal—or a rattan placemat. Build up layers of color and don't be shy about using large fabric placemats with smaller woven mats on top—it will look good once the table is fully laid.

Think about your choice of flatware, too. Nowadays, there are many different styles to choose

opposite **As the evening draws in, this table will get more colorful with the glowing chili lights and abundance of candles.**
left and below **Everything on the table—placemats, bowls, glassware—echoes the shades of autumn!**

below and right Wooden dishes and bowls work well on a Thanksgiving table. Use them to display groups of vegetables, and place smaller dishes of nuts around the table for guests to nibble between courses. Chopsticks come in all colors and shapes, and can be used at the table for purely decorative purposes. Here they create a wonderful still life at each setting, combined with artichokes and gourds.
opposite Each place setting is surrounded with goodies. Here we see a tempting bowl full of nuts alongside a satsuma and a bottle of beer to guarantee a happy guest!

from, with handles made of bamboo, wood, colored resin, and so on. Chopsticks can be colorful, too, placed alongside knives and forks for variety and decoration, or to be used for the appetizer. If you have basic steel or silver flatware on hand, tie a colorful bow on the handle of the knife and place each whole setting on a richly colored background.

Glassware in shades of red, orange, green, and yellow will work really well on this table. Scour the supermarket for interesting green glass bottles of beer and sparkling spring water. Choose candles in similar shades, and make sure everything is glowing for a truly festive experience. Bamboo-shaped candles and colored votives in colored glass holders are perfect. Multicolored tree lights and outdoor lights will also be effective and encourage the Thanksgiving spirit. If your table is by a window or doors leading outside, decorate the area you look onto with storm lanterns and lights. They will cast a warm glow as the evening draws in.

festive supper

A light meal can be turned into a festive occasion with a little effort and plenty of imagination.

There are many occasions—over Christmas, for example—where you want to share a light meal with a few friends, but also to capture the atmosphere of the season.

Silk is a great fabric for a tablecloth at this sort of occasion—it has a certain decadent quality to it, and a yard of basic raw silk shouldn't be too expensive. As it frays easily, try pulling the loose threads to create a relaxed fringed edge on the sides that don't have a selvage. Make napkins to match from any leftover fabric and, if you want to make the table covering more decorative, sew on crystal or pearl beads in a loosely scattered pattern. Sequins will work well, too.

Roses look great on a festive supper table. Try placing a rose at each setting—either integrated with the napkin or standing in a dainty glass. And add to this some interesting table gifts, such as beaded pens or tiny decorative candles wrapped in tissue paper. Float small candles in dainty cut glassware and choose some pretty placecard holders.

left **Choose unusual decorative objects as gifts for your guests, such as fragile glass balls in each water glass, clear plastic or glass droplets at each setting, or little mother-of-pearl boxes tied up with ribbon.**

this page, main This table has an almost magical quality, with the soft candlelight and pieces of dainty glassware and china. A tall dinner candle sits on an elegant drip tray with hanging droplets, and smaller candles sit in gilt wire holders and float in star cut glass in a ring above the settings.
below Sparkling glassware across the table will enhance the festive air of the occasion.
bottom Place large candles in storm lanterns or stemmed glass bowls, and surround the base with rose petals or full rose heads.

exotic christmas spread

Red, green, and gold are the traditional colors of Christmas. Employ them in unusual ways to create an exotic festive table.

Christmas is a special occasion for everyone. Though there are many possible themes for a table setting on this special day, a rich, sumptuous display will be enjoyed by all. Draw your color inspirations from the traditional decorations of red berries, green holly and ivy, and lots of gold, but adapt these themes using unusual objects and textures to make your setting a little bit different.

Try using a piece of gold organza as a table runner or buying banana leaves from an oriental supermarket and using them as a base for the setting. Exotic

opposite Red, green, and gold look gorgeous laid out on this huge banana leaf. Hanging decorations and glass votive holders carry the color scheme higher.

left An abundance of candles, gold-wrapped chocolate coins, and fruit—both artificial and fresh—make this a really festive setting.

below You don't have to have a Christmas tree—just decorate any suitable house plants.

As long as your elements fit into your chosen color scheme of red, green, and gold, you can't go wrong.

below Large wooden platters make great "lay" plates on this festive table and mark each place setting. They are topped with an organza napkin, gift bag, bowl, flatware, and festive decorations.

right A centrally positioned light fixture is a good place from which to hang decorative balls on metallic ribbon and cord.

Twist flexible ivy around mirrors and picture frames, and scatter individual holly leaves along a hearth or window ledge.

flowers are good at Christmas time as well. They are usually hardier and more durable than standard "Christmas" flowers, and there are many different festive shades to choose from. A single exotic stem will cost less than a traditional Christmas bouquet and will probably last longer. Collect holly and ivy from the yard or nearby woods, and trail it around the area to be decorated. This greenery can also be tied around the knives and forks at each setting or circled around the base of a centerpiece.

Candles intensify the warmth and festivity of the occasion—at any time of the day or night. Choose warm colors and sit altar candles on thick gold candlesticks and saucers. If you have any odd saucers or candleholders, why not invest in a can of gold spray paint and give everything a quick squirt to get into the festive spirit?

Table gifts are of utmost importance here. Make little gift bags from metallic organza and wrap tiny gifts to place as a surprise on each plate. Fortune cookies or foil-wrapped candy will look enticing. Be creative when hanging your decorations, too. A tree is an obvious choice, but light fixtures and mantelpieces are also good hanging places for Christmas decorations. And remember: even these don't have to be traditional—you could hang chocolates and fortune cookies for an unexpected twist. Just make sure your guests don't walk off with all your decorations!

below Pop a miniature ball in the wineglass at each setting and use old wineglasses to hold small candles, propped up with a mixture of glitter and decorative red sand.
right Each set of silverware has been tied together with gold string attached to a Christmas ball.

far left If you run out of suitable holders, simply put your candles in little pots of glitter for a festive display.
left These chocolates sit on a bed of crumpled clear cellophane for a magical touch.

new year's eve bash

New Year's Eve always calls for a party and is a good chance to exploit any themes that weren't used at Christmas.

Silver is always a good color for New Year's Eve—particularly if you were enjoying an abundance of gold at Christmas. Choose another color to go with the silver—pink or blue will work well—and aim to stick to these two colors.

Play around with different materials on the table top. Be funky with metal pie plates and foil takeout containers—easily found in household or kitchen departments. They will give the party a less formal "sit-down" feel, as guests pop outside to watch a firework display or leap up to play party games. Disposable napkins work well for this type of occasion, too. Make platters or mats for each setting by covering basic cork squares with tinfoil or using inexpensive foil cake pans. Iridescent glitter, clear cellophane, and lots of silver wrapping paper can be used to decorate the table top and surrounding surfaces.

Choose flowers or plants that sit within your chosen color scheme. You can buy dyed carnations or can spray white carnations with silver paint for a space-age effect, and float flower heads in a bowl with glowing gel candles.

left Layers of silver have been placed at each setting built up from a central runner made from metallic gift-wrapping paper.
above Here the colors of bright blue and silver have been rigidly adhered to to create a space-age setting. Even the sideboard has been covered in silver giftwrap to unite the whole scene.

right An elegant cocktail shaker is a practical and decorative necessity for this occasion. Glasses are all decorated with fun metallic party pieces, such as streamers and miniature glitter balls. A bead curtain makes a great backdrop.

below A fun row of blue cocktails has been decorated with a skewered piece of banana leaf topped with kiwi fruit and an olive. Keep plenty of extra cocktails ready in glass decanters to spread color across the table and to make sure top-ups aren't far away.

cocktails and canapés

A stylish cocktail party is fun to plan for a birthday, Christmas, or New Year's Eve celebration, or is a good way to liven up an ordinary Saturday night!

Plan a big buffet spread and theme everything from knives and forks to ready-prepared drinks. Here it really is the presentation that counts.

Prepare little trays of snacks presented with candles and piles of pebbles. Look for decorations tagged onto strands of pliable wire—these are great to wrap around knives and forks. Invest in a few banana leaves and cut them up to use as mats. Try layering elements, such as leaves, gravel, and candles on plates and small dishes, so each display is like a miniature "garden." Use anything flat and tray-like to serve drinks and snacks—coasters and shallow plates are ideal.

Candles in every shape and size are a must. Expand your color palette to include blue, green, and red so everything is festive and bright. Invest in brightly colored liqueurs and mixers, and you can use these as your inspiration. Shake up a few cocktails, and the party will be well under way!

above left This spread has been laid out on a circular table to provide access from all sides. Everything has been placed in multiples to give lots of choice and plenty to see. The candles will be kept alight all through the evening, and a row of colored lights adds interest to the far wall.

above A selection of pineapple cubes is served from a colorful tray. Each food offering has been decorated with candles, pebbles, and leaves—all relatively inexpensive and very effective.

the settings

Modern mealtimes tend to be rather informal, but there are occasions when a more formal setting is appropriate. A table set with row upon row of eating implements can seem daunting, but this need not be the case. Provided the table is laid correctly and you follow the simple rule of using the outermost utensil or utensils first, you can't go wrong. For this reason, a thoughtful host will lay the table carefully for a formal meal, so that no guest needs to feel embarrassed by making a mistake.

international informal

The most common setting for an informal Western meal positions the dinner knife to the right of the dinner plate with the soup spoon to the right of the knife. The dinner fork goes to the left of the plate, with the napkin neatly folded to the left of the fork. The dessert fork and spoon are then laid horizontally above the plate, the fork first with the handle to the left, and the spoon above it with the handle to the right.

1 Napkin in a simple fold
2 Dinner fork
3 Dinner plate
4 Dinner knife
5 Soup spoon
6 Dessert fork

7 Dessert spoon
8 White-wineglass
9 Red-wineglass
10 Water glass

British formal

A formal meal provides an opportunity to use lots of china and silverware. If you have a large dining table, make full use of the space by laying the dessert spoon and fork inside the dinner knife and fork, and by including a butter plate to the left of the setting. The dinner knife and fork are used together in the European style, with the fork held in the left hand, tines down, and the knife held in the right hand for cutting and for guiding food onto the fork.

1 Napkin in a simple fold
2 Butter plate
3 Dinner fork
4 Dessert fork
5 Dinner plate
6 Dessert spoon
7 Dinner knife
8 Soup spoon
9 White-wineglass
10 Red-wineglass
11 Water glass

English afternoon tea

For afternoon tea, the butter plate is placed centrally, with the napkin to the left, and the bread knife, dessert spoon, and pastry fork—in that order—on the right-hand side of the plate. The teacup and saucer are set above the flatware, with the teaspoon lying horizontally on the saucer behind the cup. The teacup handle should sit parallel to the teaspoon.

1 Napkin in a simple fold
2 Butter plate
3 Bread knife
4 Dessert spoon
5 Pastry fork

6 Saucer
7 Teacup
8 Teaspoon

American formal

This setting is for a formal three-course meal with a fish appetizer. A bread knife is optional and would be laid on the butter plate. When eating the main course, the dinner fork is transferred to the right hand for each bite, and back to the left hand when the knife is needed for cutting. Dessert utensils can also be laid across the top of the setting or brought in when dessert is served. It is not necessary to use both spoon and fork, but may be easier.

1 Napkin in a simple fold
2 Fish fork
3 Dinner fork
4 Dessert fork
5 Dinner plate
6 Dessert spoon
7 Dinner knife
8 Fish knife
9 White-wineglass
10 Red-wineglass
11 Water glass
12 Butter plate

French formal

French settings differ from American and British in a number of ways. Butter plates and knives are not used; bread is laid directly on the table, and butter is not served. Forks and spoons rest face down, and a tablespoon is used for soup in favor of the more rounded soup spoon. A knife rest is provided so the dinner knife can be laid back on the table, ready to be used for the cheese course, before dessert is served.

1 Napkin in a simple fold
2 Dinner fork
3 Dessert fork
4 Dinner plate
5 Dessert spoon
6 Dinner knife
7 Soup spoon
8 White-wineglass
9 Red-wineglass
10 Water glass

Chinese informal

For a Chinese meal, the chopsticks should be laid together to the right of the dinner plate, with the ends resting on a stand. The soup bowl and teacup are laid behind the plate, and a small dish for sauce is placed in front of the teacup. The soup spoon may be positioned in the bowl or at the side, to the left of the chopsticks. It is polite to offer guests who may be inexperienced with chopsticks the option of a knife and fork.

1 Dinner plate
2 Chopsticks
3 Chopstick stand
4 Sauce dish
5 Teacup
6 Soup bowl
7 Soup spoon
8 Saucer

Japanese informal

There are many possible settings for a Japanese meal, depending on the occasion and the food being served. For a basic setting, the rice bowl is on the left and the covered soup bowl on the right. Fried or broiled foods are served in an open plate behind the rice bowl, with a small dish for pickle at the side. A cup for tea sits at the back on the right. Chopsticks lie horizontally side by side on a stand at the front, pointing to the left.

1 Rice bowl
2 Chopsticks
3 Chopstick stand
4 Soup bowl
5 Pickle dish
6 Teacup
7 Dinner plate

Sources

CHINA AND TABLEWARE

ABC CARPET & HOME
888 Broadway
New York, NY 10003
For a store near you,
call (212) 473-3000
www.abchome.com
new and vintage linens, silverware, crystal,
tableware, melamine, dinnerware, fabrics,
and trim

ALESSI
For a retailer near you,
call (212) 431-1310
www.alessi.com
Italian-designed kitchen- and tableware

ANTHROPOLOGIE
375 West Broadway
New York, NY 10012
(212) 343-7070
for a store near you,
call (800) 309-2500
www.anthropologie.com
furniture and home furnishings

BARNEYS
660 Madison Avenue
New York, NY 10012-8448
(212) 826-8900
www.barneys.com
home furnishings and accessories

BED, BATH AND BEYOND
620 6th Avenue
New York, NY 10011
For a store near you,
call (800) GOBEYOND
www.bedbathandbeyond.com
superstore with home accessories, linens,
kitchenware, candles, and glassware

BLOCK CHINA & CRYSTAL
41 Madison Avenue
New York, NY 10010
(800) 233-9054
www.blockbasics.com
kitchen- and tableware

BLOOMINGDALES
1000 Third Avenue
New York, NY 10022
(212) 705-2000
www.bloomingdales.com

CHRISTOFLE
50 Main Street, Suite 1275
White Plains, NY 10606
(914) 328-1002
www.christofle.com
top of the line flatware, crystal, and china

CORNING/REVERE
140 Washington Avenue
P.O. Box 7369
Endicott, NY 13761
www.corningware.com
oven-to-table baking dishes

THE TERENCE CONRAN SHOP
407 East 59th Street
New York, NY 10022
(212) 755-9079
www.conran.com
furniture and home furnishings

CRATE & BARREL
1860 W. Jefferson Avenue
Naperville, IL 60540
For a store near you,
call (800) 967-6696
www.crateandbarrel.com
kitchenware, china, glassware, pottery, linens

DANSK
108 Corporate Park Drive
White Plains, NY 10604
For a retailer near you,
call (800) 29-DANSK
www.dansk.com
glassware, flatware, and dinnerware

DENBY POTTERY CO. LTD.
For a retailer near you,
call (800) DENBY-4U
www.denbypottery.com
tableware

FARBERWARE
One Merrick Avenue
Westbury, NY 11590
For a retailer near you,
call (877) 327-2932
www.farberware.com
tableware and kitchen accessories

FISHS EDDY
889 Broadway
New York, NY 10003
(212) 420-9020
For a store near you,
call (877) 347-4733
www.fishseddy.com
interesting collection of inexpensive
restaurant-type china and colored glassware

GATES OF MARRAKESH
8 Prince Street
New York, NY 10012
(212) 925-4104
high-quality furniture, candleholders,
ceramics, and glassware

GLOBAL TABLE
109 Sullivan Street
New York, NY 10012
(212) 431-5839
wonderful collection of tableware, china,
dishes, glassware, flatware, sake sets, and
unusual candles

HOME DEPOT
2455 Paces Ferry Road
Atlanta, GA 30339
For a store near you,
call (800) 430-3376
www.homedepot.com

LENOX
100 Lenox Drive
Lawrenceville, NJ 08648
For a retailer near you,
call (800) 223-4311
www.lenox.com

MIKASA
25 Enterprise Avenue
Secaucus, NJ 07094
For a retailer near you,
call (866) 645-2721
www.mikasa.com

MOSS
146 Greene Street
New York, NY 10012
(212) 226-2190
*contemporary glassware and housewares
from Europe*

ONEIDA
Sherrill Shopping Plaza
606 Sherrill Road, Sherrill
New York, NY 13165
(800) 877-6667
www.oneida.com
stainless steel and silver-plate flatware

PFALTZGRAFF
York, PA 17401
For mail order or a retailer near you,
call (800) 999-2811
www.pfaltzgraff.com
casual dinnerware and home accessories

PIER 1 IMPORTS
461 Fifth Avenue
New York, NY 10017
For a store near you,
call (212) 447-1610
www.pier1.com
*country-style furniture, baskets, candles,
candleholders, table linen, dinnerware, colorful
glassware, pottery, and home decor items*

PLATYPUS
126 Spring Street
New York, NY 10012
(212) 219-3919
*eclectic household items, kitchenware, china,
glassware, flatware*

POTTERY BARN
2488 E. Sunrise Boulevard
Ft. Lauderdale, FL 33304
(954) 565-0335
www.potterybarn.com
tableware, linen, flatware

QUONG YUEN SHIN & CO.
32 Mott Street
New York, NY 10002
(212) 962-6280
Chinese tea sets, rice bowls, and plates

REED & BARTON
144 West Britannia Street
Taunton, MA 02780
For a retailer near you,
call (800) 343-1383
www.reedandbarton.com
silverware

RESTORATION HARDWARE
1700 Redwood Highway
Corte Madera, CA 94925
For a store near you,
call (800) 762-1005
www.restorationhardware.com

SASAKI TABLEWARE
41 Madison Avenue
New York, NY 10010
(800) 233-9054
www.sasakitableware.com

TIFFANY & CO.
Fifth Avenue at 57th Street
New York, NY 10022
For a store near you,
call (800) 843-3269
www.tiffany.com

WALLACE SILVERSMITHS
175 McClellan Highway
East Boston, MA 02128
For a retailer near you,
call (617) 561-2200
www.wallacesilver.com

WATERFORD WEDGWOOD U.S.A INC.
For a retailer near you,
call (800) 955-1550
www.waterford.com
*full selection of Waterford & Wedgwood china,
glassware, lamps, and linens*

WHITE ON WHITE
888 Lexington Avenue
New York, NY 10022
(212) 288-0909
repro traditional furniture, china, and linens

WILLIAMS-SONOMA
51 Highland Park Village
Dallas, TX 75205
For a store near you,
call (877) 812-6235
www.williamssonoma.com

TABLE LINENS AND FABRICS

LAURA ASHLEY
7000 Regent Parkway
Fort Mill, SC 29715
(803) 396-7744
www.lauraashley.com

DOMENICA ROSA FINE LINENS
& ACCESSORIES
12016 Poppy Street N.W.
Minneapolis, MN 55433
(888) 354-9388
www.domenicarosa.com

FINE LINENS
1193 Lexington Avenue
New York, NY 10028
(212) 737-2123
www.finelinens.com

JACK THE RIPPER TABLESKIRTING
P.O. Box 20248
Houston, TX 77225
(800) 331-7831
www.tableskirting.com
tableskirts, napkins, and tablecloths

PEACOCK ALLEY
4311 Oaklawn #150
Dallas, TX 75219
(214) 520-6736
www.peacockalley.com
table linens

SFERRA BROS
77 Cliffwood Avenue
Cliffwood, NJ 07721
(800) 336-1891
www.sferrabros.com

THE TABLECLOTH CO.
514 Totowa Avenue
Paterson, NJ 07522
(800) 227-5251
www.tablecloth.com

CANDLES

CHANDLERS CANDLE COMPANY
For mail order,
call (800) 463-7143
www.chandlerscandle.com

COVINGTON CANDLE
976 Lexington Avenue
New York, NY 10021
(212) 472-1131
*custom-made dinner and pillar candles in
various colors and sizes*

HUDSON DRY GOODS
873 Broadway
New York, NY 10003
For a store near you,
call (212) 228-7143

ILLUMINATIONS
1995 South McDowell Boulevard
Petaluma, CA 94954
(800) 621-2998
www.illuminations.com
candles and candle accessories

YANKEE CANDLE CO.
South Deerfield, MA 01373
For a retailer near you,
call (877) 803-6890
www.yankeecandle.com

DECORATIVE PAPERS, RIBBONS, FLOWERS,
AND ACCESSORIES

B & J FLORIST SUPPLIES
103 West 28th Street
New York, NY 10001
(212) 564-6086
florist supplies

BILL'S FLOWER MARKET INC.
816 Sixth Avenue
New York, NY 10001
(212) 889-8154
artificial birds, foods, and flowers

CAPE COD CRAFTERS
Route 1
Freeport, ME 04032
(207) 865-1691
www.capecodcrafters.com
ribbons, candles, and table decorations

CARLSON CRAFT
1750 Tower Boulevard
North Mankato, MN 56003
(800) 774-6848
www.carlsoncraft.com

CORZ
910B Buccaneer Drive
Glenview, IL 60025
(847) 724-2947
www.corz.com
table decorations

CRAF-T-PEDLARS
1009-D Shary Circle
Concord, CA 94518
(877) PEDLARS
www.pedlars.com

CRANE & CO.
30 South Street
Dalton, MA 01226
(800) 268-2281
www.crane.com

GABRIEL EDITIONS
P.O. Box 633
New York, NY 10021
(800) 998-1133
www.gabrieleditions.com

JAM PAPER
15 Hudson Avenue
Tenafly, NJ 07670
(201) 567-6666
www.jampaper.com

KATE'S PAPERIE
561 Broadway
New York, NY, 10012
(212) 941-9816
www.katespaperie.com

PETALS
For a store near you,
call (800) 920-6000
www.petals.com

THE RIBBONERIE
191 Potrero Avenue
San Francisco, CA 94103
(415) 626-6184
www.theribbonerie.com

WILLOW TREE LANE
For a retailer near you, call
(877) 665-3084
www.willowtreelane.com
invitations and accessories

ARCHITECTS AND DESIGNERS WHOSE
WORK IS FEATURED IN THIS BOOK

CUNNINGHAM FURNITURE
43 Davisville Road
London W12 9SH
UK
t./f. +44 (0)20 8743 1972
m. +44 (0)7957 468790
Pages: 52–54

ELIZABETH BLANK
Floral & Interior Designer
77 Regents Park Road
London NW1 8UY
UK
t. +44 (0)20 7722 1066
Pages: 96–99

TAG ARCHITECTS
14 Belsize Crescent
London NW3 5QU
UK
t. +44 (0)20 7431 7974
Pages: 122–125

ROBERT DYE ASSOCIATES
Design Consultants/Chartered Architects
39–51 Highgate Road
London NW5 1RT
UK
t. +44 (0)20 7267 9388
f. +44 (0)20 7267 9345
info@robertdye.com
www.robertdye.com
Pages: 104–107

MOOARC
198 Blackstock Road
London N5 1EN
UK
t. +44 (0)20 7354 1729
www.mooarc.com
Pages: 5, 50–51, 58–61

LEVITT BERNSTEIN ARCHITECTS
1 Kingsland Passage
London E8 2BB
UK
t. +44 (0)20 7275 7676
f. +44 (0)20 7275 9348
www.levittbernstein.co.uk
Pages: 7, 70–73

Picture credits

5 the Rowlands family's house in London designed by MOOArc; 7 Aggie Mackenzie's kitchen in north London designed by Matthew Goulcher & Levitt Bernstein, built by LAD Construction; 8–9 Marian Cotterill's house in London; 50–51 the Rowlands family's house in London designed by MOOArc; 52–54 kitchen designed and supplied by Cunningham Furniture; 56–57 Sophy Hoare's house in London; 58–61 the Rowlands family's house in London designed by MOOArc; 66–69 Clare Mannix-Andrews's house in Hove; 70–73 Aggie Mackenzie's kitchen in north London designed by Matthew Goulcher & Levitt Bernstein, built by LAD Construction; 74–75 Clare Mannix-Andrews's house in Hove; 76–79 Ros Fairman's house in London; 82–85 Marian Cotterill's house in London; 92–95 Stephan Schulte's apartment at York Central in London; 96–99 an apartment in London designed by Elizabeth Blank; 100–103 Marian Cotterill's house in London; 104–107 Robert & Lucinda Dye's house in London designed by Robert Dye Associates; 112–115 Marian Cotterill's house in London; 116–119 Sophy Hoare's house in London; 120–121 Ros Fairman's house in London; 122–125 house in Hampstead designed by TAG Architects; 128–129 Stephan Schulte's apartment at York Central in London.

Index

Figures in *italics* refer to captions.

acknowledgments

First and foremost I would like to say thank you to David Brittain for his incredible and unfailing visual talent, support, and friendship. Thanks also to Mark Kirk, who kept us laughing, and to Catherine Randy for lots of things, including her fantastic design skills and dedication.

Thanks to Debi Treloar and Louise Leffler for introducing me to Ryland Peters & Small, and to Gabriella Le Grazie for giving me such an enjoyable and inspiring opportunity. Finally, thanks to Sophie Bevan for her wonderful way with words.